E^6 Excellence

Expect

Engage

Equip

E^6

Educate

Evaluate

EQ + P

How to coach and consult individuals and teams by putting your house in order.

Jim Gulnick, BSEE, MBA, I/O Psych
Lisett Guevara, BSIE, MSIE, D.Ed.

Cover Design: Rafael Guevara

Photgraphy: Amer Chaundhry, New Jersey, www.amer-fotografia.net

1st Edition: U.S.A (2018)

www.90daysolutions.com
Editing: Jim Gulnick
ISBN: 978-1-941435-08-3

Editorial:

90daysoulmate.com, LLC

Table of Contents

1 The System

Milgram, in his experiments on obedience to authority, shows that individuals tend to conform to authority due to situational variables that promote conformance and obedience to an authority figure despite the harm or damage they might do to another human being. These controversial experiments have been repeated and supported by other experiments and research that corroborate his findings. Humans tend to give over their decision-making power, logic, and reason to the control of a higher authority if put in certain authority/subordinate roles.

Milgram's world-renowned experiment of obedience to authority was to try to understand if normal people would obey authority and conduct harmful impersonal experiments on test subjects. His experiment design was to have an experimenter-authority figure give commands to the participant-teacher that would have them inflict increasingly higher levels of electrical shock, beginning at 15 Volts and increasing to 450 Volts at 15 Volt jumps, on the confederate-learner if they answered questions incorrectly. Interestingly enough, Milgram went through great efforts to create a simulated shock machine that was so real looking that it fooled two electrical engineers (Russell, 2011). The learner was separated from the teacher and strapped into a chair in another room.

Methodology

Milgram had participants believe that they were randomly selected as either a teacher or learner in a supposed experiment to test a new method of teaching/learning. In the first official experiment Milgram conducted, the participant would become a teacher and was required to shock the confederate-learner who purposefully answered word-pair questions incorrectly and then bang on the wall at only the 300- and 315-Volt shocks (Russell, 2011). The participant-teacher would sometimes protest or try to stop the experiment but was told that they must go on. No physical manipulation or forceful coercion was used – just verbal requests and authoritarian orders. If the participant-teacher raised greater concerns and was reluctant to continue, the experimenter-authority would command the participant-teacher to go on in increasingly stern directives (Navarick, 2009).

Results

Milgram wanted to learn if, by pure obedience to authority through situational factor manipulation, he could get the participant-teachers to complete all levels of shock issuance and finish the experiment. The research question was if the participant teacher would stop the test or obey the experimenter-authority. The result was that 65% of the participants gave shocks all the way up to 450 Volts.

Milgram used a meek looking learner and a stern looking intellectual authority figure to attempt to get the highest completion rate possible (Russell, 2011). The results show that situational attributions can strongly trump dispositional attitudes and opinions. The environment of a laboratory, the importance of an experiment and study, and the perceived authority and trust in soothing, calm, reassuring voice can have people put their decision making strategies on hold while accepting some greater good. The benefits override the potential harm and the ends justify the means.

Part of the success of the experiments has been as much the acting and sensationalized production as the study itself (Reicher & Haslam, 2011). The experiment can show us how easily we can be moved to do things that harm others and justify these actions through outside control. But, the experiment can also show authority how better to control the general public. Have we learned to be wary of authority, or have we gained useful insight into how authority can better control the public? It is interesting that current research suggests continued support for Milgram's findings.

Discussion

Navarick (2012) suggests that there are three stages in a decision-making process of a participant in whether to withdraw from an experiment. The stages are priming (collecting evidence), decision (mental), and choice (action). Priming is where the participant is affected by the negative situational factors magnified by things such as proximity of the learner and salience of the evidence such as level of direct distress witnessed through visual and auditory feedback. The decision stage is where the teacher decides to go on or stop. An important point in this experiment is at the initial plea from the learner to stop. It appears that if the teacher agrees to go on at that point it somehow reduces the stress by making a decision to go on and provides a basis of consistency for the teacher to go on all the way until the end (Navarick, 2012). The choice stage was when the teacher had to decide if the benefits of the experiment and their consistency of action up to that point outweighed the potential harm to the learner. Navarick (2012) suggests that the stress of verbally arguing with a proximate authority may be greater than the stress of harming a remote learner and that the act of shocking the learner each time dulled the teacher's internal objections.

Corroborating Research

Others experiments focused on individuals who defy unjust authority and do the right thing. Bocchiaro & Zimbardo (2010) studied what individuals were thinking during the time they decided to disobey the unjust authority to learn about what traits and thoughts went into disobedience to authority. The experiment put the participant in the role of a coach who would provide escalating verbally abusive statements from a preset list to a confederate acting as a performer solving a problem. In this experiment 30% of the participants provided the full list whereas 70% stopped and would no longer follow the authority's requests. The main reason people disobeyed was that they made a spot decision that doing the right thing and stopping outweighed the penalty and they also thought what they did would have been typical. They top reasons for stopping included concern for the well-being of the performer, and morality and inconsistency of continuing the experiment in light of the pleas to stop. In support of Milgram's findings, the experimenters found that the coaches tended to go all the way to the end of the experiment if they continued on past the first plea to stop by the performer.

Conclusion

In conclusion, current research supports Milgram's findings. The trumping of dispositional attitudes and internal values by situational stimuli cause people to do the unthinkable. People tend to be obedient to authority, even if unjust, due to situational inputs and the influence of authority. Much of the obedience is based upon the roles of those involved and the situational framework of the experiment. When we see someone as an authority figure, we tend to rely upon their judgment over and above our own. We figure that they know what they are doing, and we tend to question our own judgment.

An interesting item for further study is to determine if our archetypical representations of authority give more weight in our compliance and obedience. For example, if the experimenter-authority wore gym shorts and a Hawaiian shirt rather than a lab coat, then would rates of obedience change? Or, if the experimenter-authority was much younger or older than the participant-teacher, then would that influence the outcomes? And lastly, if the participant-learner were to be a large physically threatening specimen would we perhaps stop at the first request? It seems probable that many things have to be in place for obedience to occur, but it also seems far easier to gain compliance from an unknowing public than one would hope. The system is the situation.

2 Integrating Coaching and Consulting

This paper will discuss how individual coaching, group coaching, and organizational consulting differ and how they work together to form an integrated solution. Each type of specialization may have distinct approaches to helping clients. The applied practices of each are unique, and valuable perhaps only to an individual, group, or organization but not all three. This paper will investigate how industrial and organizational psychologists adjust the processes and approaches they utilize as they provide coaching and consulting services to individuals, groups, and organizations.

Coaching and Consulting Overview

Coaches work with individuals to find strengths and the right fit in careers to achieve that next level of success. Coaches work with building teams to help form them around a good range of member capabilities and help the team through the stages of team development to smooth out the transition to high performance groups. Consultants work with organizations to implement change though systems analysis and holistic approaches.

An increasing amount of contemporary theories suggests the learning organization is able to constantly improve to increase its competitive advantage (Lowman, 2002). As of 2009, 70% of surveyed U.K. companies utilized coaching with 44% offering it to all of their employees (Segers, Vloeberghs, Henderickx, & Inceoglu, 2011). That is a firm majority of companies in the U.K. and the world is seemingly moving towards a future with coaching firmly entrenched in organizations. This coaching focuses on beneficial behaviors, performance optimization, and personal development (Segers, Vloeberghs, Henderickx, & Inceoglu, 2011). Coaching helps people develop valuable job-related habits, set and achieve goals, and live a balanced life.

The integration of coaching and consulting occurs when individuals are coached, teams are guided, and organizations consulted in a deep and broad development and change program. Integration flows through all levels when there is an organizational-wide, continuous-learning, and consultant-directed change program adopted by the company, embraced by the leaders, and inculcated throughout the culture.

The Role and Strategies of Individual Coaching

Individual coaching helps employees gain insights through career counseling. Choosing effective and dependable psychological and skill-based assessments to properly evaluate people helps coaches understand the client's best available career choices and evaluate what it may take to move to that next position. Assessments help to show strengths and what additional training is required to have a high-probability of success, overcome concerns, and be directed to best fit jobs.

The Clifton StrengthsFinder and The Five Factor Model are two psychological evaluations that may also give and employee an edge in self-confidence. The Clifton StrengthsFinder is a frequently used personality questionnaire which helps individuals to understand their own talents and strengths (Onishi, 2005). The Five Factor Model has been shown to be helpful in accurately predicting work association, type of job or career, and the status and happiness received for women over a 50 year longitudinal study (George, Helson, & John, 2011). Self-assessment can help a person understand fit, potential for success, and likelihood of job satisfaction. Self-knowledge can lead to self-confidence and a more externally expressed confident leader who followers are willing to follow.

Self-aware individuals become autonomous learning and achieving machines capable of determining the directional, strategy, and feedback mechanisms required when taking responsibility for their own success (Powell, 2011). Self-knowledge brings clarity to one's role in life and the contribution that can be made to the world we live in. Besides the benefit of focus, self-knowledge helps build congruency in thoughts, beliefs, and action leading to a fulfilled and energized life.

The Role and Strategies of Group Coaching.

Group coaching is all about team building. The primary reason for developing work teams within an organization is to increase the effectiveness of the workgroup (Lowman, 2002). The organization's climate can be evaluated from the standpoint of the employees in the workgroup setting and how they feel in relationship to team effectiveness (Lowman, 2002).

The group coach uses 360° feedback and self-assessments with potential team members to help pick the best mix of individuals from a workgroup perspective. Members must bring together a broad set of skills and abilities and not just come from different departments.

Four stages of team development that are widely utilized in human resource training are based on Tuckman's model of group development and consist of forming, storming, norming, and performing (Bonebright, 2010). Team development training can be provided before a team is formed in order for the potential members to understand and become familiar with the challenges and stages of team development. Challenges in each of the stages need to be addressed and worked through with the help of the coach.

Looking at teams from a systems theory standpoint, they require a purpose, methods to carry out tasks, role definitions, and the ability to utilize their knowledge to accomplish the work they have committed to carry out (Lowman, 2002). These organizational teams need to be purpose focused, process directed, people connected, and performance measured to ensure desired result has been met.

Although attracting the right teammates is important to an extent, having the proper team framework in place, putting in support systems, and focusing on team effectiveness provides the biggest benefit for the buck.

The Role and Strategies of Organizational Consulting

Bertalanffy developed systems theory from an organismic biological approach where an entity can be evaluated from different perspectives to give a clearer picture of the whole (Drack, 2009). An organization can be looked at as a system formed from a complex group of symbiotic variables including values, processes, structure, attitudes, and behaviors (Lowman, 2002). The system reacts with its environment and changes to grow and overcome challenges. Systems theory breaks down organizational frameworks into a series of subsystems defined as purposive, methodological, operational, and psychosocial oriented systems which each define a different dimension of the organization (Fuqua & Newman, 2002).

The subsystem view of the organizational is not an attempt to break the organization up into tiny disparate parts but to make sure a number of diverse perspectives are evaluated to make sure nothing is missed. When all subsystems are addressed, the effect on the whole is greater than the sum of the parts.

Organizational consultants are very interested in an organization's internal circumstances that lead it into a climate of change, the steps needed to work through it, and the readiness of the organization for positive change (Bouckenooghe, Devos, & Van den Broeck, 2009). There are a variety of frameworks and new processes that need to be put in place to support the desired positive change applied through a consultation (Lowman, 2002). From adopting new equipment and procedures, to clarifying roles, goals, and rewards, organizational transformation needs to take hold throughout the organization in support of the consultation.

The best method for assessing organizational needs is to conduct a diagnostic audit. The diagnostic audit consists of collecting inherent organizational information in order to create a background abstract including the purpose of the consultation; developing a detailed overview of each of the organizational subsystems including its structural configuration, policies, and finances; documenting the flow of information, communication, and processes; and interpreting how the organization sees itself and the its relationships with others (Lowman, 2002).

Organizational climate change can be gaged by assessing the implementation and presence of team support systems through the Supports Systems Survey and by administering the Perception of Team Performance (PTP) which rates team effectiveness on a number of items (Lowman, 2002). The climate changes as a result of systems being put in place and employees recognize their own effectiveness operating within the new systems.

Without systems to support the changes in place, organizations tend to slide back to where they were before the consultation. A positive and supportive organizational climate encourages higher work satisfaction, promotes employee efforts, and increases length of employment (Xiaobei, Frenkel, & Sanders, 2011). Employee positive perspective of change and system effectiveness is related to the presence of support systems (Lowman, 2002).

From Individual Coaching to Organizational Consulting

Individual, group, and organizational coaching and consulting should be treated as an integrated program of change. Individuals with diverse psychosocial needs form specialized task groups within an organization having a clearly defined purpose for its existence. Working within each of these entities simultaneously provides the greatest potential for positive organizational change that is adopted and lasts.

The Roles of Leadership are Constantly Changing

Transformational leadership focuses on the needs of the followers and works through a continuous change process to help followers develop to their maximum potential (Du, Swaen, Lindgreen, & Sen, 2013). Contemporary leadership theory is synonymous with contemporary approaches. Contemporary approaches impact and develop more leaders throughout the organization than traditional individualist great-man approaches. Transformational leadership requires that the organization is transformed at all levels including individuals and groups.

It is central for the consultant to measure the difference after implementation to organizational wide systems. Support systems need to be in place to maintain the change so that the consultant knows they have made a difference and have a greater likelihood of success. Measuring the organization's climate change helps provide needed proof to keep individuals, groups, and the organization on track during its mission and aids in the effectiveness of the change program.

Conclusion

This paper discussed how individual coaching, group coaching, and organizational consulting differ and how they work together to form an integrated solution. Each type of specialization may have distinct approaches to helping clients. From individual assessments utilizing intelligence and skill testing, to The Five Factor Model of personality and Clifton StrengthsFinder, coaching and counseling individuals helps them to be more successful in jobs that match each individual's strengths while learning to live a balanced life.

Individual coaching, group coaching, and organizational consulting are helped by choosing effective and dependable psychological and skill-based assessments to properly evaluate people, place them in supportive groups, and structure the best possible systems for successful change. Team development benefits from using 360°

feedback and self-assessments to place individuals in mutually beneficial work environments and groups. The organization as a whole is helped by the consultant utilizing system theory and diagnostic audits to get at the heart of company issues.

Industrial and organizational psychologists adjust the processes and approaches they utilize as they provide coaching and consulting services to individuals, groups, and organizations in a manner consistent with the needs of each specific entity. Industrial and organizational psychologists need a broad and deep chest of assessment and analysis tools to derive the biggest benefit from eager clientele.

3 Dispositional Personality Determinants

Personality determinants are somewhat elusive and universally questioned. Some psychologists believe that much of an individual's personality is inherited through the genes of the individual's ancestors. Other psychologists suggest that personality is established bit by bit through experience within the social environment.

The purpose of this paper will be to discuss to what extent genetic factors, environmental factors, or an amalgamation of the two regulate the development of personality.

Overview

Nature or nurture, which is the question? Theories which support genetic inheritance of personality suggests people are born with certain traits, while theories which support environmental personality development suggests people develop these traits over time. Theories that support genetic development of personality suggest that personality is born into a person and supply innate core characteristics which are highly immutable. Theories which support environmental influences on personality development presuppose that personality is developed and learned behaviors which are treatable and malleable.

Genetics as a Determinant of Personality

Traits that are consistent over time are part of the genetic makeup of the individual. Trait theory supported the genetic factor as a personality determinant. Stimuli evoke behavior and responses in which traits are identified and revealed (Ryckman, 2013). Traits are seen in the behavioral tendencies exhibited. Allport identifies traits as an actual part of the brain body system where stimuli are turned into responses according to the trait expression (Ryckman, 2013). Thus, the capacity and tendency to act or behave in certain ways are built into the person and brought to light by situational context and inputs. Traits were considered permanent and lifelong aspects of behavior (Ryckman, 2013).

Cattell defined personality as the way a person acted in a certain situation, personality traits can be inferred, and behavior can be predicted (Primi, Ferreira-Rodrigues, & Carvalho, 2014). The personality traits evaluated in Cattell's 16PF model are fairly consistent over time (Primi, Ferreira-Rodrigues, & Carvalho, 2014). Cattell's 16 global factors of personality ended up contributing to the first version of the widely acclaimed Five Factor Model of personality (Primi, Ferreira-Rodrigues, & Carvalho, 2014).

Freud's most important contribution in personality development is his proclamation that people are driven to act unconsciously by aggressive and sexual instincts which makes him sound like a proponent for genetic factors in personality development. However, Freud builds from the innate to the environment in his theory of personality development.

Environment as a Determinant of Personality

Freud suggests that innate and pre-programmed impulses cause us to act based upon early childhood or unconscious programming meant to fill unfilled desires or urges (Ryckman, 2013). Personality organization comes from the need to balance tension between basic raw impulses and societal standards of acceptable behavior (Marcia, 2006).

This is where Freud's theory of id, ego, and superego emanate. Freud's psychoanalytic theories lead to therapy and the connection of adult behaviors with early childhood memories. Freud's personality development focused on psychosexual development where trauma induced during different stages of childhood sexual development lead to adult issues (Ryckman, 2013).

Neo-Freudian theories built upon the psychoanalytic theory of Freud suggesting and proposing the environment as a determining factor of personality.

Horney agreed with Freud in the role of childhood in the development of adult patterns of behavior but disagreed with his theory of psychosexual development (Ryckman, 2013). Horney postulates that neurotics through unfavorable family, social, cultural, and environmental conditions are alienated from their real self and instead try to achieve everything, gain all knowledge, and like everyone (Ryckman, 2013). Horney's theory is abstract, difficult to test, but appears to be useful in application and treatment with patients (Ryckman, 2013).

Bowlby's attachment theory builds off of Freud's steps with the benefit of new empirical and theoretical strategies (Shaver & Mikulincer, 2005). Bowlby's theory proposes that humans are born with a psychobiological system that seeks protection and security from real or perceived attachment figures and the types of interactions with these figures at various stages of life corresponds with patterns of predictive outcomes which program behavior (Shaver & Mikulincer, 2005). Confirmation and disconfirmation of these working models can help change attachment orientations in patients (Shaver & Mikulincer, 2005). This theory is complex, an explanation that can benefit therapists, provides much material to be further studied and researched, and yet cannot be said to be accurate.

Erickson believed as Freud that development follows a set of universal stages but focused much more fully on the role of the ego and its continued growth and impact throughout a lifetime as a result of successful or unsuccessful resolutions to life's crises (Ryckman, 2013). Erickson's stages of development continued throughout life with each having different impacts on personality development. Erickson offers a comprehensive yet abstract and highly untestable theory that has provided vast influence and benefits in personal and business psychology and has continued to generate interest amongst scholars (Ryckman, 2013).

Adler proposed that present actions are dictated by objectives for the future or views of the ideal-self in comparison to Freud's view that innate patterns and programs create behavior (Ryckman, 2013). Adler agrees that parents play an essential role in the development of patterns of behavior but he is less deterministic in their singular attribution or contribution of these programs on behavior (Ryckman, 2013). Adler suggested that people follow either constructive or destructive paths to superiority ascribing to behaviors or lifestyles classified as ruling, getting, avoiding, or being socially useful (Ryckman, 2013).

Jung disagreed with Freud's theory that sexual drive is the predominate creator of personality (Ryckman, 2013). Freud's focus was on analysis of neurosis while Jung was on individual psychology in the pursuit of spiritual fulfillment (Taylor, 1998).

Both Freud and Adler utilize their fundamental theories in the explanation and treatment of neurosis in individuals. In all cases, theories give possible reasons for behavior, and as long as the patient believes in the theory, then treatment offers the potential for healthy results. Delusional psychologists providing delusional theories to delusional patients may result in positive outcomes just as hundreds of religions create behavioral frameworks without the necessity of all being the least bit accurate. While Adler's theory is comprehensive, it is difficult to test and validate (Ryckman, 2013). Apparently with psychological theory, the blusterier the proponent, the less provable the theory and underlying concepts.

Bridging the Gap

Personality is developed as environmental impacts genetic predispositions. Although personality psychology may have started with Freud and progressed through the neo-Freudians, today's research has focused on more testable trait research with less complex theory and more valid and reliable results such as the five-factor model (Shaver &

Mikulincer, 2005). Complex theory provides the foundation for research and condensation into simpler more generalizable theories that can be tested.

Psychoanalytic theory suggests that traits are changeable. There is support for suggesting that traits are able to be changed and that behavior can be therefore modified with intervention (Magidson, Roberts, Collado-Rodriguez, & Lejuez, 2014). With intervention, patients are able to be helped, reprogrammed, and problematic behavior may be altered (Magidson, Roberts, Collado-Rodriguez, & Lejuez, 2014). Psychoanalytic theory gives hope to those suffering from abnormal behavioral tendencies seeking help. Since therapy can change personality and behavior, therefore environment can impact personality and guide it.

Conclusion

Personality determinants are viewed by various psychologists at difference phases of personality development. Much of an individual's personality is genetically inherited and continues to be established step by step over time through experience within the social environment. Both genetic factors and environmental factors regulate the development of personality.

4 Innate Goodliness

The idea of innate good has been argued and discussed by psychologists and theologians. Although discussed ad nauseam, the question of its existence resists conclusion and therefore continues to be discussed along with the theories of personality. This purpose of this paper is to discuss the idea of innate good through the view of trait, biological, humanistic, and behavioral theories.

Innate Bad

In the film Natural Born Killers by Oliver Stone, a major theme is the role of nature versus the media environment in human violence (Withers, 2012). The film suggests that the main characters are born evil while at the same time media sensationalism provides reinforcement to the violent acts perpetrated. Whether a person is born bad or good, environmental conditions may influence personality and behavior. If all people were born good, then goodness would exude from every corner of the earth, evil would not be known, and genetic predispositions for harmony, love, and resolution would envelop the universe. For a moment, let's investigate a world where people were innately good.

Trait Explanation for Good

Trait theory suggests people are born with certain traits. Trait theories would suggest that a tendency for good is born into a person and these innate characteristics are rather permanent. Stimuli evoke behavior and responses in which traits are identified and revealed (Ryckman, 2013). Traits are seen in the behavioral tendencies exhibited. Allport identifies traits as an actual part of the brain body system where stimuli are turned into responses according to the trait expression (Ryckman, 2013). Thus, the capacity and tendency to act or behave in certain ways are built into the person and brought to light by situational context and inputs.

If a person is born good in a somewhat permanent manner, then good behavior would ensue no matter the stimuli. Psychoanalytic theory suggests that traits are changeable and thereby innately good people could become evil. Evidence supports the malleability of traits and resulting modification of behavior (Magidson, Roberts, Collado-Rodriguez, & Lejuez, 2014).

Dispositions, such as innate goodness, are thought to be intrinsic preferences for behavior that are with the individual since birth and stay with an individual over a lifetime. Jung thought that introversion and extroversion were innate dispositions that would be contoured by a person's interactions over time with the environment and situations that they encountered (Ryckman, 2013). Allport believed that dispositions were personal personality traits that affected individual personality organization (Ryckman, 2013).

The most significant impact is that personality traits are measureable and predictive of future behavior. The question is always if personality traits are innate or developed over time. The question of nature or nurture lingers. But whatever the case, if someone were innately good, this personality trait should be a precursor to ensuring behavior tendencies.

Biological Explanation for Goodness

Eysenck believed that character, temperament, intellect, and physique were relatively consistent over a lifetime and were what made up a person's personality (Ryckman, 2013). Eysenck called these items that made up personality "traits" and designated them as stable and enduring (Ryckman, 2013). But, where did these traits originate? Eysenck hypothesized that the central nervous system (CNS) was the root determiner of introversion and extroversion differences in individuals (Ryckman, 2013).

Personality may develop from a Multimodal Matrix of Contributors (MMC) which consist of biological induced traits, social and cultural influences, and patterns and programs learned through family and environment impacts throughout childhood (Georgakopoulou, 2013). Quite simply, a child is born with an innate set of personality traits that seem to be founded in the central nervous system and learn other socially induced personality behaviors as they develop. Personality is both a product of biology and social influences.

Cattell suggested that traits are relatively permanent tendencies that tell a person what to do when confronted with a present situation (Ryckman, 2013). Cattell proposed that both constitutional traits (biological traits) and environmental traits (experience traits) give rise to both nature and nurture components to personality (Ryckman, 2013). It has be theorized that some personality traits such as goodness are born into the very nature of a person.

Research has shown a connection between personality and unique characteristics of the central nervous system. Biological dissimilarities found in items such as the dopamine receptor genotypes were found to be tied to the Big Five personality dimensions (Cam et al., 2010). With support of present research, biology and social influences contour personality and to that extent the possibility that goodness is biologically rooted.

Humanistic Introspection to Become Good

Humanistic theories are based upon the assumption of an inborn development apparatus that will move an individual towards realizing full potential if environmental circumstances are optimum (Ryckman, 2013). Maslow believed in order for an individual to begin the process of attempting to become self-actualized, basic needs would first have to be met (Ryckman, 2013). Without the basic needs being met, people would never approach self-actualizing attempts. Students lacking food, water, shelter, or safety were not able to focus on the long-terms benefits of higher education and needed to first remove these hindrances from blocking grasp of long-range success opportunities (Rich, 2011). It is hard to think long-term, act benevolent towards others, or just be nice when short-term survival instincts feel threatened. Perhaps goodness blooms only after basic needs are met?

Rogers proposed that emerging individuals who trust in their own experience and self-concept were few and far between (Ryckman, 2013). Although people may have known what was instinctively good for them, society and environmental impacts were not congruent with self-concept and resulted in what Rogers thought was person that was not fully functioning (Ryckman, 2013). Rogers believed that if people could be led to a congruent view of past experiences with self-concept through a therapist's unconditional positive regard, then a more organismic view will be perceived and they would be more psychologically strong (Ryckman, 2013).

Allport thought that a person was in the state of becoming and all behavior was controlled by internal forces (Ryckman, 2013). Humanistic theory presupposes that humans have worth and should be valued and the direction of growth is towards psychological health (Ryckman, 2013). Allport also suggested that people had inherent religious orientations to help them understand their observations and experiences (Ryckman, 2013).

The innately driven growth process which leads to achieving human potential is self-actualization (Ryckman 2013). The idea is that when people make their own choices and control their own behavior they will become all that they can be and live according to their own plan. Unfortunately, there is very little proof that internally directed processes derived from one's own thoughts would be moral or lead to a similar set of valued behaviors if they were not socially controlled (Ryckman, 2013).

Humanists argue that science and empirical research threatens the ability to research humanistic theory because is diametrically opposed to what is needed to study personal growth and the worth of people (Ryckman, 2013). Humanistic psychology has not been able to provide adequate research and empirical studies because much of the research is qualitative and not quantitative (Rennie, 2012). Even the qualitative research studies conducted have not been presented well by the humanistic psychology and have been relegated to non-mainstream outlets (Rennie, 2012). Humanistic psychology does little to answer the question of innate good.

Behavioral Control to be Good

Skinner suggested that we are conditioned by our environment and events external to us (Ryckman, 2013). Operant conditioning is when we make a connection between the behavior in a given situation and the results we obtain (Ryckman, 2013). Furthermore, Skinner proposes that components in his theory are situational event, the behavior that ensues, and the situation or consequence that result from the behavior (Ryckman, 2013). It would only be the positive reinforcement to good behaviors that would keep a person acting good whether they were innately good or not.

Skinner's theory has been used by politicians to induce people to do what is good for them and to control populations by setting consequences that direct behavior toward an end good despite the free will of the public (Hocutt, 2013). The idea here is that people may believe they have free will but the choice between the stick and the carrot leads them to choose the carrot every time. Free will is maintained in the mind of the actor, however, the behavior is preordained by the situation and consequences. Innate goodness yields to controlled behavior.

Rotter's expectancy-reinforcement model suggests that the behavior chosen is based upon what one expects to get for doing it times the anticipated likelihood of receiving it (Weiner, 2010). Rotter pointed to skill and chance as the internal and external causes of action (Weiner, 2010). An internally focused person may determine outcomes are a product of their doing while externally oriented person may say luck determines outcomes. It comes down to the extent at which someone perceives to have an internal or external locus of control.

According to Bandura, self-efficacy is the confidence someone has in their own ability to execute a task or skill (Saville et al., 2014). Self-reference, social interactions, and evaluative feedback are a few of the factors that shape a sense of self-efficacy (Saville et al., 2014). Bandura suggests that skill practice experience, social feedback, indirect involvement with others, and held emotions are important factors in the development of self-efficacy (Saville et al., 2014). I would suggest, how you feel about yourself, how others evaluate you, how you interact and compare with others, and how you feel when performing a task help lay the foundation for self-esteem and self-efficacy as well as the reinforcement of good actions.

Conclusion

Innate good was reviewed through the view of trait, biological, humanistic, and behavioral theories. Good behavior may be a trait brought about through genetically controlled biological functions. Self-actualization may move one towards an innate goodness as the struggles of survival vanish leaving one at peace and open to giving and receiving at a higher level. Goodness may be controlled through external forces which reinforce good behavior. Finally, whether innate good exists, its trait based, biological residing, self-actualizing, or socially controlled exhibition depends on all personality constraints and catalysts. Goodness must reside internally, we must know its existence, our basic needs must be satisfied, and others must reinforce its display for goodness to be evoked.

5 Performance Appraisal Tools to Identifying Training and Development needs in Organizations

Performance appraisal tools most effective at identifying training and development needs in the organization need to be accurate and fair. The tools must measure objective results-oriented behaviors that are directly derived from the job analysis and flow from organizational goals. In reality, they should build from the criteria discussed in the structured job interview or found in the job description and be clearly reflected in the expectations and objectives set for the employee at the beginning of the year. The criteria should be valid and reliable measures of job performance in line with organizational objectives.

When an employee's tasks are set to achieve objectives, which are aligned and support organizational goals, then evaluating the performance of the employee to determine training and development needs directly impacts the attainment of organizational targets. For instance, if an employee who is a business development specialist is tasked with bringing on new customers, the objective criteria could include number of customers and actual amount of sales. Actual numbers could be set at the beginning of a time period and the evaluation could assess how the employee met these goals along with rest of the items that are part of the evaluation.

In terms of fairness, the perception of the evaluated employee is key. The employee expects both the process of appraisal and the treatment received from the appraiser to be fair (Clarke, Harcourt, & Flynn, 2013). Performance appraisals are often involved in discrimination litigation and as such evaluations need to flow from processes that are organizationally objective and fair to the individual (Martin, Bartol, & Kehoe, 2000). Without fair processes and fair treatment, the most effective appraisal tools subject the organization to legal ramifications.

Procedural justice includes encouraging employee feedback, removing bias, maintaining consistent evaluation process, treating employees fairly and truthfully, and providing decision justification (Martin, Bartol, & Kehoe, 2000). Using valid and reliable measures determined from the job analysis, including outcome focused objective and subjective criteria, training evaluators, and discussing results with employees help in the methodological and perceived fairness of the performance appraisal (Werner & Bolino, 1997).

In conclusion, valid and reliable measures of job performance that are evaluated and discussed fairly with employees can provide the most effective platform for determining training and development needs in line with organizational objectives.

Evaluating Training Programs

The most important assessment of new hire training programs is evaluation of learning criteria. It is very valuable to assess whether the new hires know the material that was introduced. Behavioral criteria evaluation is important as well, but it is more helpful in addressing ongoing training needs for these new hires. Of course, these evaluations go hand-in-hand. Organizations want trainees to feel good about the training, learn the material, apply in on the job, and achieve the desired results for the organization. It may be useful to address all criteria to assess future training requirements.

Over 50 years ago, Kirkpatrick published a series of articles where he described four levels of training criteria used to evaluate training program effectiveness (Alliger & Janak, 1989). Reaction, learning, behavioral, and results are the four Kirkpatrick's evaluation criteria that may be used in an effort to evaluate the overall successful transfer of knowledge leading to behavioral change and results through an organizational training program (Saks & Burke, 2012). Each assessment criteria helps an organization evaluate the different dimensions of training. From how the training was received or if the trainee learned, to if behavioral changes were made and if the organization obtained the results it expected may be evaluated using these criteria.

How did the trainees feel about the training?

Reaction criteria focuses on improving the content, design, and delivery that helps in making positive changes to the program (Saks & Burke, 2012). Reaction criteria was based on the reaction of the trainee in a emotional sensing of how much they liked or how they felt about a training program (Alliger & Janak, 1989).

Did the trainees learn the material?

Learning criteria helps understand whether new hires are learning the material and if content or delivery change would be useful (Saks & Burke, 2012). Learning criteria is a more facts based evaluation surrounding the absorption and application of the relevant facts and messages delivered within the training program (Alliger & Janak, 1989).

Are the trainees using the material on the job?

Behavioral criteria evaluation helps determine the extent of which new hires are applying the training and making use of what they learned (Saks & Burke, 2012). Behavioral measures are looking at the extent trainees put to use the material within the program on the job (Alliger & Janak, 1989).

Did the training provide the expected results?

Results measurements helps an organization determine the impact training is having on the organization and if the expected results are being realized (Saks & Burke, 2012). The results evaluation of the training program measures the impact that the organization received by conducting the training such as productivity improvements, attitude improvements, or cost reductions (Alliger & Janak, 1989).

Identifying an Employee's Training Gaps

The performance appraisal is the best method to evaluate performance and identify an employee's training gaps (or the gaps in the training). Utilizing a combination of management by objective, 360-degree reviews, and self-reporting, the gap between where the employee is currently and where the organization needs them be can be assessed. Why this method would be useful is that it would address three areas of concern:

1) Assessing the attainment of preset goals and targets to determine what is missing
2) Gaining feedback on ability to work with others, communication, and teamwork
3) Self-Analysis/Career objectives for employee development

A training needs assessment helps takes into account the needs of the organization, the employee's current abilities, and career development (Iqbal & Khan, 2011). The assessment includes determining the tasks and associated proficiencies required for the job and comparing the present ability level of the employee in the position (van Eerde, Tang, & Talbot, 2008).

Training gaps can been found in areas where the employee performance is lacking or in an area in which the employee wants to further develop for the future career opportunities. The performance appraisal should be based on the job and task analysis as well as what would have been in a structured interview for a new hire. These objective goals will have conveyed to the employee at the beginning of the year. These are the targets by which to manage expectations, results, and measurement towards objective.

Kill the Performance Appraisal

Performance appraisals and thereby the tools used are dangerous, biased, and unnecessary for an organization. According to Total Quality Management (TQM) theory, the success or failure of an organization is due to the system and not the people. Measuring performance against objectives creates animosity and resistance. Performance appraisals kill organizations as they create fear, foster short-sighted practices, and thwart teamwork (Aluri & Reichel, 1994).

TQM stresses process optimization as well as performance improvement (David, 2012). The management of knowledge within the organization is used to promote competitive advantage. Knowledge management requires the development of employee evaluation and reward systems to promote desired behaviors that create customer satisfaction (David, 2012). It is the system that is responsible for setting the environment for performance.

However, performance appraisals for a majority of organizations are based on targets that are only believed to impact the business such as number of client visits, dollar amount of quotations created per year, and sales volume. The problem most organizations have is that what really matters in long term value creation and success is highly elusive. Therefore, what is measured are things that can be measured and are assumed to be predictive of organizational success.

Most organizations do not have an understanding of systems, motivation, or what really matters and turn to ineffective performance appraisals which result in poorly performing systems (Crow, 1996). What is measured is a matter of convenience leading to focusing on output rather than fixing problems and this measurement promotes a fallacious view of employee responsibility while excluding the system (Aluri & Reichel, 1994). If there is a problem with the workforce, then the system needs to be improved for it is the system that is responsible for individual performance (Aluri & Reichel, 1994).

Embrace the Training Appraisal

It becomes clearer that employee training programs should be appraised to determine the level of effectiveness the programs have for the organization. Focusing on the teaching rather than the learning is an effective way to increase intellectual capital and not at the expense of human emotion. Performance evaluations like structured interviews can be stressful as well as leave employees feeling criticized.

What if the organization took responsibility for the success of its business through the systems it managed rather than the people it employed? Instead of have performance reviews, there would be training assessments where the target for performance improvement of the measurements evaluated would be the content, delivery, and transfer of knowledge or impact on increase of intellectual capital. Systems rather than people would be evaluated for bringing quality products and solutions to customers. Data would be collected to fix the system, not to fix the people.

System problems must be improved as they are responsible for individual performance (Aluri & Reichel, 1994). Total Quality Management (TQM) promotes system streamlining through thorough system assessments to optimize employee performance (David, 2012). Employee training as a performance system would be evaluated and assessed with the end result being a better system for delivering content and information to employees.

What if the organization took responsibility for the success of its business through the systems it managed rather than the people it employed?

6 Emotional Intelligence and Facial Emotion Research

Facial Emotion Perception Ability (FEPA) has been extensively examined in relation to those with mental illnesses and brain abnormalities (Demirbuga, Sahin, Ozver, Aliustaoglu, Kandemir, Varkal, Ince, 2012; Diehl-Schmid, Pohl, Ruprecht, Wagenpfeil, Foerstl, & Kurz, 2007). However, few researchers have examined FEPA in non-clinical participants (Chen, 2014; DeBusk & Austin, 2011; Wojciechowski, Stolarski, & Matthews, 2014). In the little research that does exist, researchers have linked certain personality traits to FEPA (Bishop, Jenkins, & Lawrence, 2007; Canli, Sivers, Whitfiled, Gotlib, & Gabrieli, 2002; Ewbank, Fox, & Calder, 2010; Mitchell, 2006). One potential avenue that may demonstrate the use of FEPA in non-clinical populations is in more adequately measuring Digman's (1990) five-factor model of personality, which included five categories of personality: neuroticism; conscientiousness; openness to experience; agreeableness; and social skills (Guido, Pino, & Frangipane, 2011).

Some researchers have noted that test takers can reliably predict their outcomes on current measures of the five-factor model (Furnham, 1997); nevertheless, workplaces continue to distribute them to determine personality types and worker aptitude (Sackett & Walmsley, 2014). Thus, a gap in the literature exists regarding a reliable method of determining Big Five personality traits. Identifying the relationships between personality factors and FEPA may provide an avenue of development that could reliably identify individuals with appropriate fundamental skills such as recognizing the emotional state of others, lead to developing training and interventions through personality training that could increase emotional facial recognition, and possibly further contribute to individuals' workplace success.

Background of Personality Tests

In the workforce, personality tests are frequently used to examine the aptitude of workers, whether for hiring or promotion purposes (Morgeson et al., 2007). Researchers have demonstrated that the ability to recognize other's emotions through verbal and nonverbal cues can affect work performance and leadership abilities (Emmerling & Golman, 2003). Recently, scholars, such as Sackett and Walmsley (2014), have begun to tout the use of Digman's five-factor personality model as a method of measuring workplace aptitude. Often, these personality traits are measured through the Big Five Inventory (BFI) instrument for personality measures.

However, the newfound celebration of the model in identifying workplace aptitude may ignore previous research, which has suggested that current measures of this personality model can be easily predicted by the test taker, particularly for the traits of agreeableness, conscientiousness, and neuroticism (Furnham, 1997). In evaluative contexts, researchers have demonstrated that workers score higher in agreeableness, conscientiousness, and emotional stability than they would if not under evaluation (Vecchione, Dentale, Alessandri, & Barbarenelli, 2014). Together, these results suggested that the BFI could be faked to demonstrate positive qualities. In order to maintain the practice of using personality traits within non-clinical populations, a more reliable measure of determining these traits is required.

Facial Emotion Perception Ability

One method that may provide such results is the use of facial recognition of emotions, or FEPA. Primarily, facial recognition tests have been applied among samples of people with mental illnesses (Demirbuga et al., 2012; Diehl-Schmid et al., 2007). Overall, facial expressions, body language, and verbal cues provide the evidence that allow us to make an evaluation of the emotional states of others (Proverbio, Calbi, Manfredi, & Zani, 2014). The premier, validated instrument for measuring FEPA, the Brief Affect Recognition Test (BART), is easy to administer, comes in electronic format, and takes relatively little time for test subjects (Diegl-Schmid et al., 2007; Dodich et al., 2014; Roberts et al., 2006). BART is a validated instrument with high test-retest reliability (Roberts et al., 2006) Thus, the proposed study will utilize BART, pending email permission from the creator, in an attempt to assess the relationships between BART and five-factor model scores.

Researchers have historically examined the traits of apprehension, extraversion, and anxiety on FEPA, to various effects (Bishop et al., 2007; Canli et al., 2002; Ewbank et al., 2010; Mitchell, 2006). The study is needed because additional validation of the overlap between the five-factor model and FEPA can potentially pave the way for better measurement of personality traits. Identifying the relationships between personality factors and FEPA may provide an avenue of development that could reliably identify individuals with appropriate fundamental skills such as recognizing the emotional state of others, lead to developing training and interventions through personality training that could increase emotional facial recognition, and possibly further contribute to individuals' workplace success. Thus, further investigation of how the five-factor model of personality may be related to FEPA using BART is warranted.

Theoretical Foundations

Digman (1990) noted that individuals' personality traits could be characterized into the following traits: openness, conscientiousness, extraversion, agreeableness, and neuroticism. Together, these traits have positive value in predicting a person's overall workplace performance (Sackett & Walmsley, 2014). Specifically, Sackett and Walmsley (2014) noted that conscientiousness and agreeableness were highly sought-after traits from employers, and also predicted an individual's performance in the criteria of negative work behaviors, extra-role work engagement, and satisfactory work completion. Although the five-factor model has demonstrated scientific validity among research populations (John & Srivstava, 1999), researchers suggest that individuals can predict the results and score higher on positive attributes when under evaluation (Furnham, 1997; Vecchione et al., 2014).

Review of the Literature/Themes

In order to examine the research related to this subject, several fields of research need to be addressed. Included in these areas of interest are Emotional Intelligence (EI), Facial Emotion Perception Ability (FEPA), and the five-factor model of personality. In addition, the current research that connects these areas will be discussed, including the current relationships that have been found between EI and the five-factor model of personality; between EI and FEPA; and between FEPA and personality.

"Universal" Facial Expressions

Facial Emotion Perception Ability (FEPA): Early literature posited that facial display of emotions was universal (Ekman & Friesen, 1971), though conflicted literature reflects that cultural and situational differences in facial emotion may or may not exist (Chen, 2014; Debrot, Cook, Perrez, & Horn, 2012; Gendron et al., 2014; Kayyal & Russell, 2013; Mobbs et al., 2006). Tested by BART, FEPA has been utilized extensively in clinical settings, though researchers are expanding this examination to include normative populations (Chen, 2014; DeBusk & Austin, 2011; Dodich et al., 2014).

Five-factor model of personality: Digman (1990) developed the five-factor model of personality, which included five categories of personality: neuroticism; conscientiousness; openness to experience; agreeableness; and social skills. However, individuals may be able to fake their scores for better outcomes (Furnham, 1997; Vecchione et al., 2014)

Relationship between FEPA and personality: Mitchell (2006) determined that a link existed between Apprehension personality traits, measured through the 16-factor personality model, and recognition of most emotions, and between Dominance, Self-Reliance, and Apprehension and the identification of fear. Researchers examining neuroscience data have found that anxiety traits are related to increased identification of fear and anger (Bishop et al., 2007; Canli et al., 2002; Ewbank et al., 2010) and between extraversion and identification of happiness (Canli et al., 2002).

Opportunity for Further Investigation

It is not known to what degree or extent the Big Five personality traits can predict FEPA. Although the Big Five personality test is a premier method of predicting performance within business settings, current methods of measuring it are insufficient and lack consistency (Furnham, 1997; Sackett & Walmsley, 2014). Overlaps between FEPA and personality traits (Bishop et al., 2007; Canli et al., 2002; Ewbank et al., 2010; Mitchell, 2006) suggest that there may be a relationship between these constructs, but the studies researched and reviewed revealed no studies that examined these two factors in conjunction with each other. Since BART, unlike current instruments of Big Five personality traits, holds little likelihood of false or faked results so long as disseminated within a specific culture, demonstrating a relationship between the two constructs may help to better identify and classify non-clinical people, including for applications within the workforces (Dodich et al., 2014). Thus, the problem that the proposed study will address is the lack of a consistent, accessible method of measuring personality (Dodich et al., 2014; John & Srivastava, 1999).

Research Questions, Hypotheses, and Variables

The purpose of proposed research is to determine if personality, as measured by the five-factor model of personality, has a statistically significant association with FEPA. It is not known to what degree or extent the Big Five personality traits, and the Big Five personality traits in conjunction with one another, can predict FEPA. This leads to the proposed research questions:

R1: Is there a significant association between agreeableness and Facial Emotion Perception Ability?

H01: There is not a significant association between agreeableness and Facial Emotion Perception Ability.

HA1: There is a significant association between agreeableness and Facial Emotion Perception Ability.

R2: Is there a significant association between conscientiousness and Facial Emotion Perception Ability?

H02: There is not a significant association between conscientiousness and Facial Emotion Perception Ability.

HA2: There is a significant association between conscientiousness and Facial Emotion Perception Ability.

R3: Is there a significant association between openness-to-experience and Facial Emotion Perception Ability?

H03: There is not a significant association between openness-to-experience and Facial Emotion Perception Ability.

HA3: There is a significant association between openness-to-experience and Facial Emotion Perception Ability.

R4: Is there a significant association between neuroticism and Facial Emotion Perception Ability?

H04: There is not a significant association between neuroticism and Facial Emotion Perception Ability.

HA4: There is a significant association between neuroticism and Facial Emotion Perception Ability.

R5: Is there a significant association between extraversion and Facial Emotion Perception Ability?

H05: There is not a significant association between extraversion and Facial Emotion Perception Ability.

HA5: There is a significant association between extraversion and Facial Emotion Perception Ability.

R6: Is there a significant predictive relationship between the Big Five personality traits (agreeableness, openness-to-experience, neuroticism, and extraversion) and Facial Emotion Perception Ability?

H06: There is not a significant predictive relationship between the Big Five personality traits and Facial Emotion Perception Ability.

HA6: There is a significant association between the Big Five personality traits and Facial Emotion Perception Ability.

Big Five personality traits may be linked to employee personality. In this research, the goal is to investigate the strength of association between the Big Five personality traits and Facial Emotional Perception Ability (FEPA). The study will also investigate which of the Big Five personality traits best predict Facial Emotional perception Ability (FEPA).

Predictor Variables – Personality Measures (Five Factors Model – Continuous Scales)

- Agreeableness
- Conscientiousness
- Openness to Experience
- Neuroticism
- Extraversion

Significance of this Subject

Potentially linking FEPA and the five-factor personality model creates opportunity for selection, training, and increased performance in organizations. Multiple researchers have noted that connections between personality and FEPA existed, but these studies have primarily been conducted from a deficit model, wherein participants overrepresented negative personality traits, such as anxiety (Bishop et al., 2007; Canli et al., 2002; Ewbank et al., 2010). These findings may lay the groundwork for contributing to increased understanding of the relationship between personality and FEPA in normative populations and allow for more reliable measurement of the five-factor traits that may contribute to workplace success (Sackett & Walmsley, 2014).

This subject contributes to the literature on the conceptual framework by potentially linking the five-factor personality with FEPA. It may also enable the accessible and consistent measurement of personality. Currently, researchers suggested that measures of the five-factor model can be faked (Furnham, 1997; Vecchione et al., 2014). Correlating the factors of five factor personality traits and FEPA may therefore address the issue of a lack of consistency in organizational research related to the five-factor model.

This subject will contribute to practice by providing a method of measuring five-factor personality traits that is not tied to self-reporting methods and relies on valid instruments linked to the established bodies of literature related to FEPA. Tapping into these traits, either as a screening method or to determine professional development opportunities, via previously established paradigms and instruments would allow measurement of the five-factor model to become more accessible in practice. For example, if a relationship is demonstrated between FEPA and the five-factor personality model, employers could distribute FEPA to employees as an accessible predictor of five-factor personality traits, and potentially job performance, in line with research by Sackett and Walmsley (2014). By reviewing this information or implementing training designed to increase FEPA, companies may reap the benefits of increased work success and job performance (Ahangar, 2012; Khokar & Kush, 2009; Sathya Kumar & Iyer, 2012).

Conclusion

Emotional intelligence is a predictor of job performance. The ability to recognize emotions in others, within situations, and in our self, leads to managing our emotions and those implicit in the situations to get better results from all involved by changing the situation for those involved. Facial emotion perception ability may predict emotional intelligence.

7 Hiring Practices

The process of determining who to hire is valuable according to the level of its validity (Hunter, & Schmidt, 1998). If the process is full of errors, not reliable, and has low validity, then the organization receives lesser performance that otherwise may have been predicted and benefitted from by using more valid approaches. Because of the applicant pool variability, the higher the reliability of the measure, the better able to predict performance and create a greater benefit for the hiring organization (Hunter, & Schmidt, 1998). The reduction of error increases the reliability and the validity.

Where do employees fit best?

Measurement

Measurements were not always as reliable, and the results of assessment procedures varied from one organization to another. The theory of situational specificity was developed which indicated that validity varied when utilizing the same assessment procedures to measure and predict performance because of subtle difference in what was thought to be the same job in slightly different settings (Hunter, & Schmidt, 1998). Meta-analysis allowed the combining of validity estimates across studies to correct for sample error variation to provide additional clarity of the average operational validity and reduce error (Hunter, & Schmidt, 1998).

Reduce Error through Additional Measurement

The value of a selection method comes down to its predictive validity and directly impacts the economic value added to the organization (Mount, Oh, & Burns, 2008). The method of measuring General Mental Ability (GMA) is a valid predictor of job performance and the strongest of all other approaches as intelligence as a construct is clearly understood and researched in depth (Hunter, & Schmidt, 1998). If there were procedures and measurements that could be added to the measure of GMA to increase its validity, then the organization would benefit from using these methods. Perceptual speed and accuracy increased the validity of GMA by 15% and is a highly valid predictor of job performance (Mount, Oh, & Burns, 2008).

In conclusion, reducing error, increasing reliability, and providing greater validity provide incremental benefits to an organization and the value created through its chosen methods of employee selection.

Situational Assessment to Increase Validity

The benefit of any selection method is the ability to accurately measure and correctly predict future performance which for many organizations may decline with time (Caldwell, Thornton III, & Gruys, 2003). The top ten reasons for predictive erosion include planning issues, poor job analysis, ineffective dimension construction, and untrained assessors inaccurately documenting unprepared candidates (Caldwell, Thornton III, & Gruys, 2003). There are so many areas subject to creating error in the selection process that validity would be wise to be questioned.

An assessment offering a significant prediction of job performance is a situational assessment. Situational assessments put candidates in a constructed situation in order to observe how the candidate deciphers the situation and for the assessor to document how the candidate behaves. For a situational assessment to be carried out and provide meaningful results a few steps must be taken. The candidate needs to know they are being evaluated, relevant situational clues must be readily available and straight forward to understand or assess, and as a result, candidates are expected to exhibit behaviors consistent with the individual's KSAs and founded on the demands of the situation (Jansen et al., 2013).

Assessment of situational demands were significantly related to job performance ($r = .27$, $p < .05$), indicating candidates who were better performers in the situational assessment received higher performance evaluations from their managers (Jansen et al., 2013). The situational assessment enables direct witnessing of a candidate's KSAs in action as well as the candidate's ability to determine what is needed in a given situation. The validity of this approach helps reduce error in the selection process. Of course, the assessment would need proper planning, flow from a thorough job analysis, and be conducted by trained assessors accurately documenting prepared candidates.

Personal Interview

Personal interviews may be a useful tool in selecting candidates and structured interviews provide for better validity than unstructured interviews. Psychological characteristics, social skills, and mental capability assessed through personal interviews can predict job performance (Huffcutt, Roth, Conway & Stone, 2001). Therefore, personal interviews appear to provide an effective method for selecting candidates.

Although general mental ability is a predictor of job performance and is assessed quite often in job interviews it accounts for less than 20% of the differences in interview ratings (Huffcutt, Roth, Conway & Stone, 2001). General intelligence, the ability to solve problems, and creativity are routinely assessed constructs of mental capability (Huffcutt, Roth, Conway & Stone, 2001). It is not likely that general intelligence can be accurately accessed within a job interview (Huffcutt, Roth, Conway & Stone, 2001).

Validity ratings for items captured during personal interviews varied from .24 for general intelligence to .58 for creativity (Huffcutt, Roth, Conway & Stone, 2001). Why such the low rating for general intelligence? It is not likely that general intelligence can be accurately accessed within a job interview (Huffcutt, Roth, Conway & Stone, 2001). Whatever the case, personal interviews can impact selection in a positive way.

Structured interviews tend to have higher validity than unstructured interviews (Huffcutt, Roth, Conway & Stone, 2001). The point is to use structure with the personal interview. Unstructured interviews provide for less validity.

Interviews are plagued with problems however. Deception by the candidates may invalidate the process by providing a preference to low qualified applicants who just happen to have made a good impression (Hogu & Hang, 2013). It is best to therefore utilize structured interviews to get the best overall validity for personal interviews and minimize the effect of uncontrolled variables.

Professional Competencies

Competencies for the successful professional may include relevant knowledge, task related skills, interpersonal skills (perhaps emotional intelligence), and the ability to solve problems. The difficult task for an organization comes when candidates seem weak in the competencies that have been determined to be important to the organization.

Determining which competencies are mandatory, trainable, and not necessary would be important for the specific position. Organizations which utilize competency selection criteria may be early on in their usage of this selection filter and not sure of the validity or utility of the determined set of wanted characteristics or competencies. It is important to determine which competencies contribute to the employee's performance compared with which add to the organization's performance (Sutton & Watson, 2013). If they do so at all.

Competencies seem to be interrelated. All the ideal competencies chosen for manager candidates were shown to be significantly correlated and this correlation may be a result of the halo effect (Sutton & Watson, 2013). In this case, if scores were seen to be low, then they would have scored low across the board. After being hired, the same employees were once again assessed for the competencies and evaluated on their performance. It was shown that attrition was correlated with low competency scores, but overall performance was not significantly related to initial competency assessment (Sutton & Watson, 2013). The overall competency ratings of the hired employees when reassessed a year later were determined to be significantly lower than those same employees when going through the selection process (Sutton & Watson, 2013).

Expectations of the screeners and the ratings they give may be high. Candidates may have learned how to fake the interview and assessment. Reality and measurement of real-world performance may prove otherwise. If competency ratings can be linked to attrition as the study indicates, then that would be a good start for using competency ratings in selection. Although many competencies were shown to not be linked with performance, the company did learn of a few that were linked and was able to continue to use them in its selection process. The company also decided to conduct exit interviews to learn if training in the unmet competencies would potentially increase retention (Sutton & Watson, 2013).

8 Validity of Reference Checking

There has been a greater focus on reference checking as an additional method of evaluating the potential quality of hire as shown by past work experience as some studies have validated observer ratings (Hedricks, Robie, & Oswald, 2013). Asking past supervisors, coworkers, and subordinates structured questions about a candidate's work-related characteristics and job-relevant actions has been found to increase validity (Hedricks, Robie, & Oswald, 2013). The key to reference checking is in the standardized approach of asking structured questions to create a valid method of capturing performance predicting measures.

When rating candidates, there are major biases for which the reviewers need to compensate. Reviewers may provide inflated ratings, suffer from lack of consistency, and play office politics when rating candidates for a new position (Catano, Darr, & Campbell, 2007). Raters may be uncomfortable with the rating system and provide equally high ratings that do not differentiate between rated individuals (Catano, Darr, & Campbell, 2007).

Rating tools are only as good as the tool itself and the assessor. Bias might appear as an effect of ethnic or racial differences. Differences in ratings may occur as a result of overt prejudice, subtle perceptual biases of assessors, or actual performance differences which result from minority differences in work atmosphere and challenges (Wilson & Jones, 2008). Raters are plagued with problems leading to validity concerns stemming from problems such as confirmation bias where opinions of an individual are formed first and then the individual is rated according to the predisposed position (Stepanovich, 2013).

Finally, the validity of the rating tool is of utmost importance. Are the behaviors and actions being measured essential for the position and indicative of high job performance? Are the raters fully trained in a uniform manner on how to utilize the screening tools? Does each rater know how to objectively score the candidate regarding each distinct attitude, behavior, or action?

9 Competency Dilemmas

Far along the selection process there are only a few candidates left for very important and needed positions. Competency tests show that all the candidates scored poorly on the assessment for the position. At this point in the selection process, competency assessments would only be significant with large numbers of candidates. However, since the number is low, other aspects such as General Mental Ability, emotional intelligence, and psychological tests may be used as predictors of job performance and selection. This is assuming that the competencies for the position are accurate in the first place.

Developing a list of competencies using a blend of organizational strategy with task analysis may help the use of competencies in the hiring process. Attributes of competencies should be aligned with organization strategy to create task statements as objective targets for examples of relevant poor, average, and excellent job behaviors (Catano, Darr, & Campbell, 2007). Although competencies remain the same throughout the organization, the behaviors associated with the competencies would be different based upon position and organizational level (Catano, Darr, & Campbell, 2007).

Assessing the competencies can be a difficult, seldom do competency-based selection methods measure and record the impact of competency-based selection on performance following hiring, and many of these systems are not legally justified (Catano, Darr, & Campbell, 2007). Because of this, competencies could be looked at as a training opportunity and selection should move on to another more reliable and legally justified basis. It is imperative to work with each employee on an annual basis to develop the core competencies through a performance management process (Huff-Eibl, Voyles, & Brewer, 2011).

One action would be to hire three employees, put them in training together on core competencies as they start to learn their job functions. At the end of a given period, one of the three new hires could be relieved of duties. The new hires could be provided with a position description, KSAOs that are needed for the position, and a list of competencies and measures of behavior exhibiting these desired objectives. Since validity and reliability of competencies are questionable to begin with and all testing and measures are only correlations of predictability when dealing with large numbers of candidates, perhaps work samples and on the job performance review become valuable.

Sharing the details of the competencies with potential applicants would enable for a better pool of applicants (Huff-Eibl, Voyles, & Brewer, 2011). Interviewers would gain better knowledge from candidates who would be better prepared to speak about these competencies through past work experience (Huff-Eibl, Voyles, & Brewer, 2011). It would appear that if three candidates appear equally absent of competencies, it may simply be a matter of assessor rather than the candidates. It also appears that the competencies were not shared with potential applicants. I would potentially have another party conduct the assessment of the candidates after revealing to candidates the required competencies for the position.

10 Meaningful Assessment Procedures

General intelligent measures along with conscientiousness testing from the Big Five traits continue to be big determiners of future training and job performance. General intelligence and conscientiousness correlate strong with performance across a wide range of jobs and conditions (. Placing the highest scoring candidate in the area with the most difficult (Barrick, Mount, & 2013)

During job placement, the potential for work overload should be evaluated in order to reduce future work inefficiencies due to long-term work performance (Zoer, de Graaf, LuijerBarrick, Mount, Hoozemens, & Frings-Dresnt, 2012). The matching of employee skills and abilities with job descriptions that were taken from a complete and thorough job analyses help to fit the employee to the job in which they will be most successful.

The objective scoring of the structured interview may also be a good place to investigate best fit and experience of the applicant. It is with this information that level of position, training requirements, and compensation may be decided.

Psychometric and Mental Ability Tests

Numerous companies rely upon psychometric and mental ability tests as a typical input into the hiring decision making process. To many, mental ability is thought to be by far the most important factor in predicting job performance, however real-life experience has taught otherwise. Studies show that general mental ability is a predictive factor in employee performance but not necessarily the only one to be used in selection.

Nuclear power plant main control room operators' safety performance was positively predicted by general mental ability in both individual and team situations (Zhang, Li, & Wu, 2013). In highly critical and technical positions, general mental ability appears to be an important factor in the selection process.

Psychometric and mental ability tests provide objective scores which help provide predictive measures for assessing and selecting and placing candidates (Tews, Michel, & Lyons, 2010). The industrial and organizational psychologist can maximize their time and streamline the hiring process. Candidates can be ranked by scores limiting by a hurdle the number of potential candidates for a new position.

The most significant characteristics of psychometric and mental ability tests are the highly predictive nature of the tests. General mental ability (GMA) was shown to be the best overall predictor of overall job performance (Hunter, & Schmidt, 1998). Combining second predictor tests enables multivariate validity to strengthen to .60 to .65 (Hunter, & Schmidt, 1998).

Using valid tests to assess aspects of a person's strengths that are predictive of success is an efficient way to screen candidates. The organization should first conduct a job analysis where they develop a list of the knowledge, skills, abilities, and other characteristics (KSAOs) necessary to do the job. Once a thorough job analysis is completed, candidate may be screened with mental ability tests and other psychological tests.

General Mental Ability, as compared with the Big Five personality dimensions, was the only variable able to successfully predict all performance benchmarks in entry-level service employees (Tews, Michel, & Lyons, 2010). It is this successful and unsurpassed ability of the GMA testing that are most significant to industrial and organizational psychologists. The major drawback is the adverse impact that may occur as a result of implementation of these testing assessments.

Cognitive Ability

Cognitive ability tests are good predictors of job performance but yield high levels of adverse impact (Murphy, Cronin, & Tam, 2003). According to members of the Society of Industrial and Organizational

Psychology (SIOP), cognitive ability assessments should always be included in personnel selection (Murphy, Cronin, & Tam, 2003).

Job Experience

Investigations have shown that job knowledge is of higher importance than general mental ability in prediction of job performance (Stauffer, 2010). The theory suggests that general mental ability and tests that are used in the selection process may be ways of measuring job knowledge indirectly (Stauffer, 2010). Could it be that intelligence is a predictor of job knowledge and job knowledge a predictor of job performance?

The above-mentioned studies show the tendency for general mental ability to be important in the decision-making process. In fact, intelligence assessments are often utilized through employment services to help aid in the process of employee selection. At first, intelligence is placed by many as a very high-ranking variable in the decision-making process. However, what is typically noticed over time is that other factors become equally important.

Fast Walk

At some point, structured interviews may be utilized and then a team may compare answers to a series of standard questions. One company found that by adding a fast walk component to its assessment process quickly weeded out slow movers and those without pep in their step. For many employees in key positions, intelligence mattered but the ability to keep up with the work seemed to be connected with the ability to walk fast.

Clear Talk

Another thing learned overtime as one organization grew was that communication ability became increasingly important. A large number of the very intelligent applicants had a difficult time conveying information in a concise and coherent manner. At the same time, it was shown that communication skills did not equal cognitive ability. The most intelligent applicants for midlevel warehouse jobs may have had job experience in the form of time on a job, but a number also had little hands-on experience when it came to getting the work done.

Cognitive ability, job experience, communication ability, and pep-in-the-step may each play a vital role in a decision-making process. Diversity in capability and function also allows formation of well-structured work teams. Methodical planners may be mixed with urgently motivated workers to clearly lay out objectives, set milestones, and at the same time work quickly as a team to obtain them. In this way cognitive ability, while important, becomes just one of a set of important items that is viewed in the decision-making process.

Pep-in-the-step Revisited

As far as some constructs that may define "pep-in-the-step", it appears that motivation and personality characteristics might play a role. Personality traits and goal motivation are predictors of a willingness to exert an effort in the attainment of a goal (Vasalampi, Parker, Tolvanen, Lüdtke, Salmela-Aro, & Trautwein, 2014). As far as personality goes there may be a specific goal oriented trait or an achievement mindset. Conscientiousness and agreeableness have been indicated to be predictors of job performance and effort (Vasalampi, Parker, Tolvanen, Lüdtke, Salmela-Aro, & Trautwein, 2014).

Job experts can assess what "needed-at-entry" to determine what additional training KSAOs are necessary (Van Iddekinge, Raymark, & Eidson, 2011). They may subjectively assess the subject, utilize testing to determine the KSAOs to work on, or perhaps just ask the candidates for a self-assessment given the position that is being attempted to be filled. The best determination of needed training would be to assess the standardized testing that measures the KSAOs possessed by the candidate.

Once training is determined, the organization can choose candidates which it feels may have the greatest amount of success in their organization. General cognitive ability was shown to be the best overall predictor of training success (Hunter, & Schmidt, 1998). Mixing tests allows the strength of the multivariate validity to grow up to .65 (Hunter, & Schmidt, 1998).

11 Personality Tests in Hiring

An individual's success and perspective are substantially and significantly predicted by the Big Five traits (Wille, De Fruyt, & Feys, 2013). Even with that said, are the best fakers of personality assessment tests the most likely to get hired and still be successful despite their faking? What can be done about it? And, does it matter?

The problem of faking occurs in assessment tests utilized to evaluate the personalities of job applicants. Applicants understand the position they are applying to obtain and tend to answer personality assessments in accordance with what they believe the position requires. Job applicants scored higher on socially desirable characteristics than incumbents who would have been expected to score higher since they already held the position and went through the application and selection process themselves (Birkeland, Manson, Kisamore, Brannick, & Smith, 2006).

Even with the ease of faking, it is difficult to assess the level of faking on personality tests. Some psychologists accept the use of the Social Desirability scale to remove applicants although research showing the connection between faked personality assessments and Social Desirability are weak at best (Galić & Jerneić, 2013). Applicants who know the desired personality of the position easily bias their assessments towards the desired results (Inslegers et al., 2012). Because of faking, should personality tests be ignored altogether?

What if it were possible to test and assess personality and traits indirectly where the applicant was less likely to fake answers? Direct testing of the Big Five personality tests yielded higher differences in Socially Desirable personality traits between applicants and non-applicants than did indirect testing (Birkeland, Manson, Kisamore, Brannick, & Smith, 2006). Picture Story Exercises (PSE) also known as Thematic Apperception Testing (TAT) are useful as the assessor instructs the candidate to write about the picture following a set of directed questions (Gruber & Kreuzpointner, 2013). The assumption here is that the indirect approach enables personality to be assessed without allowing the candidate to fake their answers as the candidate projects their own personality onto and into the situation shown in the PSE.

Direct measures are easier to fake but easier to administer, whereas indirect measures are more difficult to implement but more difficult to fake. Is it possible to get more honest answers from candidates on direct measures testing? Candidates might be told that they are being considered for a wide selection of positions, so it is best to answer as honestly as possible to find the best fist. Objective tests appear to have more utility because of ease of administration. The drawback is that they are also easier to fake.

Faking's Impact on Validity

Faking is a thoughtful attempt to change responses to personality questions in order to create a false impression intended to fit in to a predetermined ideal set of characteristics viewed as favorable by the assessor (Arendasy, Sommer, Herle, Schützhofer, & Inwanschitz, 2011). Providing an unclear or an ambiguous set of characteristics that makes for the ideal candidate creates an environment where it is more difficult for the candidate to employ faking (Arendasy, Sommer, Herle, Schützhofer, & Inwanschitz, 2011). But, is it even important to try to reduce faking where it may have little impact on job performance prediction?

Distortion due to faking has little impact on the predictive nature and validity of personality test and uncorrelated with predicting job performance (Gibson & Weiner, 2000). Correcting faking scores did not influence the overall ranking of candidates and thus would have little consequence on hiring decisions (Gibson & Weiner, 2000). The amount of faking held no correlation to overall job performance (Gibson & Weiner, 2000).

Given the overall innocuous effect of faking, the difficulty in screening it out, and the need for efficient and effective overall placement processes, faking should not be a concern to the organization. The organization should inform the candidate that for the best overall fit in position and with the organization, it would be best to answer truthfully and honestly as the different openings require different personality types to best fit the job.

The organization could also misdirect the candidates with a personality diversity statement where it implies that positions are filled to create a mix of personalities that work best in a team environment. Perhaps an ambiguous statement of characteristics that covers many differing personalities allows a candidate to fixate on only those which are a match.

Last Word on Faking it

Faking tends to not impact test validity and therefore should not be a concern for most organizations. Since faking has little if any overall effect on predictive strength of personality assessments, is difficult to screen out, and organizations need effective placement strategies, faking should be ignored. Sure, organizations could implement projective or observed personality measures, but this would increase the difficulty in screening candidates.

Faking and its ensuing personality measurement distortions have little influence on the predictive ability and legitimacy of assessments (Gibson & Weiner, 2000). Correcting faking scores has little consequence on hiring decisions and faking itself is not related to overall job performance (Gibson & Weiner, 2000).

Faking, therefore should not be a high priority concern but does have impact on selected employee conformance with appropriate workforce behavior. If honesty, integrity, and morality traits are not targeted in selection, then high-risk taking individuals involved in abnormal and deviant workplace behaviors are more likely to participate in faking on personality tests in favor of socially desired behaviors and these individuals end up being hired (O'Neill, Lee, Radan, Law, Lewis, & Carswell, 2013). So, faking may not impact validity of the personality measures for predictive performance but may impact workforce well-being by putting social deviants on the payroll.

In conclusion, faking is a problem if desired traits predictive of position success are not balanced with honesty, integrity, and morality traits in the selection process. Potentially, strong character references from the candidate and other background checks that the hiring organization can evaluate may help the organization find quality candidates without concern for faking and its implications. Additionally, focusing on virtuous traits may reduce the risk for deviant behavior in new hires.

Cultural Fit

Fitting a candidate's personality with the organization helps attract and retain workers as well as helps ensure that employees more quickly assimilate and become valuable contributors with hire performance. It is an efficient way to recruit and helps streamline the process.

Candidates rated organizations more attractive when the personality of the potential employing organization was similar to that of the study participant in terms of the Big Five model (Green, 2011). Candidates are thought to be more favorable towards organizations that allow them to fit in with the existing organizational personality (Green, 2011). The importance of matching the personality of the candidates with the organization is that it makes the company appear more attractive to the candidate and aids in the efficiency of the selection process. A mismatch of personalities could lead to difficulty in recruiting talent when there is not a good fit between candidate and organizational personality.

Job related knowledge, skills, abilities and other characteristics (KSAOs) are important but personality may be as important, if not more important, in a making a good hiring decision. Traits such as emotional and social intelligence that help measure if an individual may fit into a workplace, will get along with others, and tend to support others from an interpersonal skill perspective can make or break a hiring decision (Hernandez, 2012).

Eighty percent of corporate hires are based upon personality match which helps determine how quickly people get along with others in the organization (Falcone, 1996). Personality tests used in hiring have shown predictive validity throughout varying organizations and performance measures (Risavy & Hausdorf, 2011). Many organizations find that proper employee selection is vital to the success of the organization. Organizations have determined that personality tests are an important part of the evaluation and utilize the Big Five model of personality which has been linked to behavioral actions that produce positive organizational outcomes (Risavy & Hausdorf, 2011).

When a candidate's personality matches that of the organization, the organization ensures a fit, creates harmony, and retains workers with higher levels job performance and satisfaction.

Personality Tests and Adverse Impact

The research by James Dakota Green on effects of matching organization personality perception with the job applicant's personality is helpful in the applicant selection process. The research pointed out the attractiveness of organizational personalities that match the personality of the candidate in terms of the Big Five model, which type of candidate is attracted to which type of organization, and how organizations can make effective use of the development of an organizational personality and then can create a brand personality strategy that better attracts and retains employees (Green, 2011).

The NEO Personality Inventory was used as a measure of the traits of the Big Five personality model to analyze potential group differences resulting from the use of personality assessments during selection of candidates utilizing different decision methods (Risavy & Hausdorf, 2011). The way the personality measures are used may create adverse impact. Using compensatory top down selection methods may provide greatest value-added return in performance (hiring utility) but create adverse impact (Risavy & Hausdorf, 2011). Adding fixed/sliding bands to the selection method may reduce adverse impact and increase company diversity by treating everyone within that band as equally qualified (Risavy & Hausdorf, 2011).

Personality tests may result in adverse impact and it is suggested that banding results into levels may eliminate the effect by treating all candidates about a certain score as equally qualified. As long as the 4/5s rule is followed and assessors are familiar with a variety of evaluation methods, personality testing can provide positive predictive results with a fair amount of utility.

12 Benefits of Youth

Younger employees have not picked up other employees' ways and approaches of behavior and thus can be directed and molded in the image that the company wants to project. Training specialists have suggested that training aimed at modifying well entrenched patterns and programs of behavior is less effective (Morrow, Jarrett, & Rupinski, 1997). Which is perhaps where the expression comes from that we all know, "You can't teach an old dog a new trick."

If a new salesperson has no preconceived habits and is given a training course, they may tend to focus on the skills learned within the course and pattern behavior on these skills since none other are known. If a mature salesperson takes the same course, then the new information must be weighed against preconceptions and habits many years in the making.

Perhaps there is a motivational aspect to training. New employees feel that they must perform to stay employed whereas tenured employees feel that the reason they have successfully stayed with an organization is that they already have the valued behaviors that the organization desires. New employees are motivated to prove themselves whereas older employees already feel proven and that training is simply a required task needed to improve those other employees.

Maintaining Development Centers

A major drawback to hiring young employees and maintaining development centers is that eventually those employees become older. Time and money have been invested to create intellectual capital that becomes a wasted asset when a company continuously turns to new employees for its future growth.

Much time and money can be spent with new employees that may not be able to rise to the challenges of the job. Instead of bringing in employees that already have proven records of success, the company is taking chances with young employees. Plus, these new employees may take the training and now as more valuable employees go elsewhere for higher pay.

The utility of management training courses was found to be generally low with some even being negative (Morrow, Jarrett, & Rupinski, 1997). I believe training specialists sometimes equate these results with older employees not being able to retain and use new material as well as younger employees, but I would rather suggest that most training departments are ill equipped to train more seasoned professionals with years of developed soft skills that have helped them make it to the positions that they occupy.

A training department at a 4,000-employee power company and recognized the complexity differences between roles such as customer service, sales, engineering, and management. Most training departments are more effective with new and younger employees in straight forward functions. Today, many companies hire younger and older workers dependent on job, experience required, and who actually applies. Some companies have found hiring more experienced workers at higher rates of pay allows them to receive greater return on investment at a faster rate.

Furthermore, what happens when a protected class is affected by disparate treatment or impact? The Age Discrimination in Employment Act (ADEA) was fashioned to prevent subjective age discrimination in employment (Siniscalco, Rahm, & Quinn, 2002). The court has held that disparate impact of even an apparently neutral hiring methodology that results in the same effect as intentional discrimination is illegal (Siniscalco, Rahm, & Quinn, 2002). Whatever filtering mechanism is to be used needs to truly be predictive of job performance to avoid disparate treatment. However, even performance predictive selection processes may result in disparate impact.

The organization exists is to create value. Value is created through the development and interplay of human capital, organizational capital, and customer capital (Mhedhbi, 2013). Human capital is valued upon its ability, attitudes, and agility (Mhedhbi, 2013). Ability and attitudes that have developed over time come from experience. Agility may be a function of youth, but it is also a function of corporate culture and the learning organization. Sure, youth can learn new tricks, but so can employees of all ages with the right type of training and development available within a learning organization.

13 Aging Workforce

Disparate treatment of employees due to age is illegal. Hiring methods that result in the same effect as intentional discrimination are illegal (Siniscalco, Rahm, & Quinn, 2002). The belief or view that "you can't teach an old dog new tricks", while based in research on reprogramming patterns of behavior, would be an indefensible position for a company to use in hiring and selection.

Training aimed at modifying well entrenched patterns and programs of behavior is less effective (Morrow, Jarrett, & Rupinski, 1997). It would be like trying to convince a manager or owner of a business that their long-held beliefs and positions are untrue and need to be reconsidered. Owners and upper management have entrenched beliefs and views that are treated like their children. They are emotionally attached to being right in their stance and would have a hard time letting go of these opinions and views. Whereas many view the younger employee as malleable and clay ready for the mold.

Older employees are human capital containing vast amount of intellectual value. Value is created through the development of human capital (Mhedhbi, 2013). Older employees already have a vast storehouse of value built within their experience. The organization throws away this value when adopting a hiring strategy that focuses on younger workers and development centers. They also are practicing illegal hiring methodology in age discrimination.

It all comes down to the selection of onboarding and training methodologies that are developed for the audience. When the training is assessed for success rather than the employee, then perhaps beneficial changes in the teaching rather than the learning will be focused upon.

Half the Workforce is over 40

The American workforce is getting older. With the baby boomer bubble growing in age, older employees are making up a greater percentage of the workforce than ever before. The number of workers between the ages of 65 and 74 doubled between 1977 and 2007 and will nearly double again by 2016 (Stack, 2013). Over half of the workforce in the United States is above 40 years of age (Winrow & Johnson, 2011).

Age Discrimination and the ADEA

Age discrimination has grown over the recent years. The number of age discrimination cases filed with the Equal Employment Opportunity Commission (EEOC) grew by approximately 50% between 1997 and 2011 reflecting an ever growing issue in the workplace (Stack, 2013). Even with additional vision on the issue, the problem has not diminished but has remained as important as ever to address and solve.

In an effort to thwart employer bias against older employees and reject the notion that job performance deteriorates with age Congress passed the Age Discrimination in Employment Act (ADEA) in 1967 (Stack, 2013). The ADEA protects older workers from discrimination through all stages of employment such as selection, promotion, compensation, and termination (Winrow & Johnson, 2011).

Even with the legislation, older workers are continued to be impacted by discrimination, biases, and false stereotypes. Companies may use an inability or unwillingness to be trained, or technological challenges as reasons to improperly displace an older employee. Whatever the reason, companies still find themselves the biased decider of worker employment, promotion, salary, and termination.

If an employer is found to have violated the provisions of the ADEA, they may face stiff penalties. Penalties on employers who violate the requirements of the ADEA can include forced reemployment, reinstatement, or promotion of the displaced worker, reimbursement of unpaid compensation, and even liquidated damages in the case of purposeful mistreatments (Stack, 2013). This means that even if a company does not intend to discriminate but unknowingly acts in ways that result in age-based discrimination there may be legal consequences.

Employee Proof

In recent decisions over the last few years, the courts have allowed employers a bit more latitude in treatment of older workers if employment decisions were made for reasonable factors other than age (Winrow & Johnson, 2011). It is up to the employee to prove age discrimination. The employee must provide evidence that age was the determining factor in the employment decision and through the "but-for test" (Winrow & Johnson, 2011). This allows employers to make employment decisions where age is a factor but not the determinate factor (Winrow & Johnson, 2011). Basically, the employee would need to provide evidence that the employment decision would not have otherwise been made but-for age. If younger workers were hired and older workers were forced out, it would need to be for far more substantial and validated reasons than perceived dedication, flexibility, and cost effectiveness of youth.

14 Best Interview Ever

The best technique to conduct a valid and reliable interview without being perceived as too restrictive includes a few minutes of rapport building, a job focused structured interview based on valid constructs, and a follow up period of questions and answers for clarity. Methods of selection based on measures of behavior stability over time such as structured interviews are valid predictors of job performance (Jansen, Melchers, Lievens, Kleinmann, Brändli, Fraefel & König, 2013). Structured interviews provide the best validity and reliability however there is an upper boundary to the strictness of structure that can be utilized in the interview before it becomes a detached, cold, and calculated process (Barrick, Dustin, Giluk, Stewart, Shaffer, & Swider, 2012).

Structured Interview

In an effort to reduce the constraining nature of structured interviews, techniques may be implemented. Rapport can be built through unstructured light conversation to calm the candidates at the beginning of the interview (Barrick et al., 2012.). Even though rapport building may effect interview validity, it is frequently used by interviewers to reduce tension and start the flow of questions (Barrick et al., 2012). Even without rapport building, the interviewer rapidly builds biases and impressions that affect the structured interview.

Research has established that in highly structured interviews, candidates who made better first impressions were presented with more offers and received better interview scores on the subsequent structured job relevant questions (Barrick et al., 2012). Whether an interviewer is involved in rapport building upfront or not, first impressions impact the selection process. Because the interviewer forms an impression which creates bias during the structured interview, then does it not make sense to ease the strain and break the ice before hitting the structured section of the interview?

Structure increases validity and reliability by focusing on information gleaned from the job analysis to establish job related constructs, asking all candidates the same questions, and measuring the responses in a uniform methodology. Allowing follow up questions by the interviewer at the end of the interview with responses and questions from the candidate allow clarification of any questions requiring further details to be recorded. The move away from the structured interview enables additional information to be learned beyond the forced questions and answers. The inclusion of the structure helps keep the focus on valid, job-related constructs, whereas the unstructured portion allows additional stones to be overturned.

Psychological and Cognitive Testing

Absent of the structured interview, psychological and cognitive testing would provide an effective method for employee selection. Psychological and cognitive assessments are useful tools for selecting employees when the methods used reliably and consistently measure attributes intended to be measured that are predictive of job performance (Ajila & Okafor, 2012).

General Mental Ability (GMA) along with Conscientiousness (CON) and Emotional Stability (ES) have a high predictive validity for job and training performance and provide important benefits in terms of utility in the employment selection process (Schmidt, Shaffer, & Oh, 2008). Meta-analytic findings indicate that two of the Big Five personality traits (CON and ES) along with GMA may be valid for predicting performance on basically every job (Schmidt, Shaffer, & Oh, 2008). Utilizing a correction for indirect range restriction, the mean validity estimates for GMA is .647, CON is .222, and ES is .124 when predicting performance (Schmidt, Shaffer, & Oh, 2008).

If assessment methods are added to the structured interview, candidates may feel that are being treated evasively or misleadingly if not fully aware of the recruitment process and the different hurdles that need to be cleared. Candidates may drop out from the process if they do not know the reason for each step and the expected outcomes. The utility of the recruitment process would need to be questioned if viable and valuable candidates were electing to no longer continue. On the other hand, perhaps the upfront testing itself is a test of the motivational factors of the candidate to stick with the process.

A meta-analysis found affective commitment to have strong positive correlations with employee attendance, performance, and organizational citizenship behavior (Sangmook, 2012). Commitment to an unclear process may enhance the employee's likelihood to remain with the organization long term. Person-Organization fit in emotional commitment results in increased job satisfaction, greater personal performance, and enhanced work quality (Sangmook, 2012). To be able to persevere through unclear times may be a benefit.

The Resume

The resume received upfront provides details of experience that could be directly relevant for the job opening. The work sample test also provides directly applicable evidence of knowledge, skills, and abilities as well as strengthens the validity of the General Mental Ability assessment.

How terrible must a recruitment process be in order for a candidate to drop out? In today's world of an employment challenged labor force where hundreds of applicants apply for every available opening, I could see this going either way. Overburdened job seekers going to extremes to find employment tossed about at the folly of organizations with ironfisted job recruitment processes. These seekers willing to go through hoops and hurdles to try to get back in the work force. Will they be fed up with the hurdles they face or embrace them like a last remaining rope hanging from the edge of a cliff? I could see this going either way…

Who do you end up with is a function of the process. Do you want to be left with those with low levels of self-esteem willing to do anything to gain employment, or do you want the employee who knows when enough is enough and has the backbone to drop out of the recruitment process? Too many assessments surrender our recruitment processes to the mindless robots who are willing to continue on despite all obstacles. Perhaps this is commitment? Perhaps this is conscientiousness?

If it is commitment, then this could be a good thing for the person and company. Emotional commitment has been shown to have strong positive correlations with employee attendance, performance, and organizational citizenship behavior (Sangmook, 2012). The fit between the employee and the organization results in greater levels of job satisfaction, performance, and work quality (Sangmook, 2012).

If continuing on with the recruitment process is a sign of conscientiousness, then perhaps it is a good indicator of future job performance. Two of the Big Five personality traits (CON and ES) along with GMA may be valid for predicting performance on basically every job (Schmidt, Shaffer, & Oh, 2008). Whatever the case, some companies have oppressive selection processes and are perhaps left with candidates who self-select to stay the course. In the long run, maybe they end up with the exact employee that fits the organization.

15 Union Environment

When faced with many candidates for an open position and a very precarious employee selection process involving union oversight, a transparent methodology with clearly defined steps needs to be carried out. It is wise to stick with valid methods of employee selection. Structured interviews are valid predictors of job performance as they take into account behavioral stability over time (Jansen, Melchers, Lievens, Kleinmann, Brändli, Fraefel & König, 2013).

All candidates must be treated fairly, given equal opportunity, and without disparate treatment or impact. With 50 candidates, four interview panels, and 45 minutes of questions, four interview panels would take less than 2 days to review all the candidates. If each candidate were given 45 minutes of questions, with a 15 minute buffer, each panel could interview 8 candidates each day and still have time for lunch. Recommended steps may include:

1) Review with the union prior to conducting the interviews the rationale, reliability, and validity of the structured interview measures developed from job analysis and performance prediction.
2) Invite and have union representatives to sit on each interview panel.
3) Provide training to all the panels simultaneously with union representatives in attendance as well as review assessment scoring procedures with all panels.
4) Conduct initial screening of candidates with each panel's goal of selecting top two candidates based upon pre-developed scoring system.
5) Create one super panel which includes at least one member of each of the four panels and two union representatives for final assessment of candidates. With eight candidates remaining, this process should take one full day with each candidate going through the 45 minute structured interview a second time.
6) Final decision made by four company representatives with union oversight.

The union's role is to ensure the job analysis fits the given position and that the descriptions are not over or under weighted or targeted towards specific candidates in the selection process ("Recruitment and selection," 2014). The union endeavors to make sure that the selection process and candidate evaluation is open to existing staff and encourages career development and opportunity within the firm ("Recruitment and selection," 2014).

If it is not possible to include union representatives in the selection process, then it is advisable to thoroughly review the selection process and selection criteria with the union as well as the members of the committee and the training that is provided. The union will expect selection of sufficiently scrutinized qualified candidates based on objective and measurable benchmarks, demand fairness and proficiency of the interview panel, and require strong, defensible scoring of the candidates ("Recruitment and selection," 2014). It is only with the union's confidence that the candidates were fairly treated, evaluated, and selected based upon valid and reliable measures that they may provide support for the results.

16 Entry Level Customer Service Position

In order to find the candidates in a fast and efficient manner for entry-level customer service positions I would consider the following computer-based assessments taken simultaneously by groups of candidates on computers separated by dividers without talking allowed between candidates:

1) General Mental Ability
2) Five Factor Model of Personality
3) Emotional Intelligence

It is suggested that an objective review and measurement of each candidate's speed, accuracy, and attitude be documented while involved in the computer assessment. Lastly, the top candidates could also provide a work sample where they were put into a simulated real-life situation to be assessed in a group setting with the pressures of a simulated work environment.

Training was provided to customer service personnel in a utility company that would deal with customer power outages, past due bills, and other service issues. There were a number of things that would be looked to develop further with customer service personnel:

- Ability to connect and communicate with others in a clear and concise yet caring way
- Positive outlook in the face of adversity, getting on the customer's team
- Problem discernment through analytical and logical steps indicative of strong cognitive ability
- Emotionally intelligent framing of problem, solution, next step, and deadlines
- Solution oriented with confident resolution and follow up procedure, knowing when to end call

Intelligence and Personality

General Mental Ability (GMA) positively predicts job and training performance (Schmidt, Shaffer, & Oh, 2008). The Five Factor model (FFM) of personality offers some insights into behavioral aspects of customer service personnel. Customer service personnel should be pleasant, dependable, responsive, and polite – all features of two of the traits of Conscientiousness and Agreeableness (Brown, Pratt, Woodside, Carraher, Cash, 2009). Twenty two percent of the difference in customer service job satisfaction is accounted for by The Big Five traits of Openness, Agreeableness, Conscientiousness, Extraversion, and Emotional Stability (Lounsbury, Foster, Carmody, Kim, Gibson, & Drost, 2012).

Emotional Intelligence

Emotional intelligence plays a huge role in the success of customer service personnel. Customer service transactions with higher levels of emotional intelligence displayed by the provider lead to higher levels of reported customer service satisfaction (Kernbach & Schutte, 2003).

Objective Measures

Monitoring the speed, accuracy, and attitudes of candidates while they take the assessments is beneficial. The behavioral traits exhibited during the stress of assessment are based on the same dispositions that predict similar behavior and attitudes on the job. While candidate reactions to job assessments do not appear to affect assessment validity they do appear to predict job behavior (McCarthy, Van Iddekinge, Lievens, Kung, Sinar, & Campion, 2013).

Work Sample Assessment

Finally, work sample assessment can help catch any glaring issues and provide a measure of real-world success in a role play situation. This may be another casual measure of Extraversion and General Mental Ability but perhaps a good way to give the candidates a taste of what the work environment would be like. In this way, candidates may self-select to not continue on with the process if they are unhappy with the prospect of interacting with customers every day in a sociable setting where mental ability, emotional intelligence, and communication are key.

17 New Hire Workplace Counseling

New employees have a difficult time assimilating into the organizational culture quickly because they are struggling to learn the required tasks while at the same time they do not have the same developed contacts of existing employees. The two most important issues blocking assimilation for new IT hires for USAA Insurance was the difficulty of work and the unclear environment in which the new employees interacted (Leidner, Koch, & Gonzalez, 2010). These workers suffered from limited professional experience within the company and no social connections within the company (Leidner, Koch, & Gonzalez, 2010).

Two ways to help achieve faster cultural assimilation is through training and mentorship. Formal training, on-the-job opportunities, and taking part in self-directed, formal, or professional development activities can help employees feel more competent and comfortable in the new organization (Haliru & Kabir, 2011). Mentoring through being assigned a teacher, guide, or collaborator, facilitates dialogue and enables the new hire to develop skills and connect within the social structure of the organization faster (Haliru & Kabir, 2011).

Cultural fit increases commitment, raises performance, and reduces attrition (Ghorbanhosseini, 2013). When an organization helps a new employee assimilate into the organizational culture quickly through teamwork and development activities, the new employee's organizational commitment is strengthened (Ghorbanhosseini, 2013).

There is need for employees to function effectively and the need for organizations to make new employees feel welcomed. The methods to use to achieve these goals are important for companies to keep in mind, however it is a cause for wonder to think about to whom this advice really applies.

If you look at various companies, you will see a big difference in the hiring and onboarding practices of all. Some companies require employees to follow an intricate training program consisting of online courses, interactive office tasks, and group trainings. Other companies bring on employees and they begin work immediately. Sometimes I believe most articles and textbooks are written with the large company or franchise in mind because many smaller companies cannot afford to invest upfront on training and assimilation efforts. They expect performance or end the relationship with the employee quickly. Perhaps they should take heed and listen to the recommendations of the Industrial and Organizational Psychologist despite the perceived upfront costs and delays in performance.

Since properly trained and culturally assimilated workers perform better and enjoy work more, assimilation delay is reduced, and the company profits long term. Person – Organization (PO) fit increases commitment, raises performance, and reduces attrition (Ghorbanhosseini, 2013). When a company facilitates cultural assimilation and provides the necessary development activities, new employees exhibit greater organizational commitment (Ghorbanhosseini, 2013).

18 Hiring Proactive Employees

So, what exactly is the benefit of hiring proactive employees? Proactive employees not only perform at higher levels but employees exhibiting proactive traits can change the constraints of the organization and thus the task structures as well. Employees with proactive personality receive benefits such as increased task control and organizational support while at the same time getting a reduction in organizational constraints (Li, Fay, Frese, Harms, & Gao, 2014).

No one would deny that proactive employees are assets to organizations. As such, how can these high performers be retained? Individuals with proactive personality traits will tend to stay with an organization if they perceive the organization provides support and commitment as well as communicates the importance of the employee to the organization (Prabhu, 2013). These seem like the same logical steps the organization would help retain any valued employee. Which brings me back to my point, many of these studies seem to be backing up common sense with statistical evidence to prove the hypothesis correct in the first place.

Proactive Personality Compared with the Five Factors Model

Proactive personality measures may be used for selection where specific behaviors such as innovation, contribution, and communication of recommendations for improvement against disagreement from others is desired. As a contextual performance measure, proactive personality is predictive of certain desired performance related behaviors supporting organizational functioning, and not of overall job performance (Crant, Kim, & Wang, 2011). The Five Factor Model has been shown to be a valid and reliable measure of job performance whereas the proactive personality measure is more predictive of specific job related behaviors that may also have a performance impact – depending on the job and requirement for innovation and need for expressing of opinions despite conflict.

A good amount of proactive personality is addressed within the Five Factor Model. Proactive behaviors variance has been shown to be up to 71% explained by openness, extraversion, and conscientiousness (Rodrigues & Rebelo, 2013). Although proactive personality measures explain 1% of variance in overall performance above the Five Factor Model, no real selection benefit is received in terms of economic utility for the organization (Rodrigues & Rebelo, 2013).

In summary, I would not recommend using proactive personality measures on their own as a selection tool. The Big Five stills wins in scale as far as reliability and validity are concerned. I could see augmenting the selection process with proactive personality measures only if specific behaviors of high innovation and open communication are desired, however, the measures of openness, extraversion, and conscientiousness can provide a good prediction of the same traits.

Effectiveness vs. Validity

Should organizational objectives determine effectiveness and not validity and reliability under potentially different conditions?
The comfort level of the interviewer and interviewee are important to more fully assess the candidate than the structured interview allows. It allows qualitative conversations to be brought into quantitative based interviews. Uncomfortable structure doesn't allow a natural flow of conversation. Unstructured interviews allow additional dimensions of a candidate to be examined however may reduce validity and reliability measures as the structure becomes compromised.

The unstructured interview may add to the structured analytical assessments for knowledge, skills, ability, such as cognitive ability, job knowledge, personality, and integrity tests. That being said, could not a structured interview be used to assess these personal dimensions so at least each candidate is treated similarly? Are there certain traits that make for better employees? For instance, perhaps the company is looking to understand the complete person to see if they fit with the corporate culture.

What can you more fully understand about a candidate during an unstructured interview that would weigh favorably or unfavorably in the decision process? Once you determine these qualities or traits, could you not create a seemingly unstructured interview that follows structure? Or, is the point to have a non-directional conversation to determine if you like or dislike a candidate based upon feelings and emotions? At the end, the decision needs to be based on something. And if it is, that something should be able to be measured.

Interviews should be all about job-relatedness in terms of the necessity to focus on the requirements of the job as dictated within the job analysis and consolidated in the job description. One company tested such structure for the first time by conducting three structured interviews with candidates facilitated by an interview group made up of a Plant Manager, VP of Operations, Human Resources Manager, and Engineering Director. Everyone was on board with the structure of asking the same 10 job related questions whose answers were rated on a scale of 1 to 5. A 1-score means the candidate did not have that knowledge, skill, or ability and a 5-score meaning that the candidate had essentially the same knowledge, skills, and abilities that were being sought after for the position.

Being able to compare candidate answers to job related questions allows companies to make job knowledge, skill, and ability focused choices. Validating results is very important. As experience is gained, job performance can continue to be assessed more accurately and job interview answers can be better related with results and predicted performance. As always, making sure testing is job-related is key. For instance, assessment testing for candidates to ensure responsibility and safety requirements have been met must be job-related (Muckle, Plaus, Henderson, & Waters, 2012).

Attitude on Job Performance

Not discussed up to this point is the importance of employee attitude on job performance. It is argued whether or not if attitude can be trained or requires much greater in-depth program to facilitate even slight changes. There is a saying, "Hire attitude, train skills." However, creating the right situation to induce the most beneficial environment to foster good attitude can only help.

If attitude is a predictor of performance, then finding workers with the best attitudes would be important. If attitudes are part of the developed and mainly innate personality of the individual, then is not the Five Forces Model which assesses conscientiousness, agreeableness, emotional stability, extraversion, and openness to experience a better method of focusing on hiring the right attitudes rather than on training attitudes in the future?

Training can provide reasons, understanding, and set situational atmospheres and environments that allow and evoke dispositional response from employees. Training cannot fundamentally and robustly change underlying dispositions to enable a change in reactions to the same stimuli. However, the stimuli can be reframed in the mind of the employee to evoke a different preprogrammed response.

On the other hand, it is possible to stretch and flex the developed attitudes of adults. Older adults completing a 16-week training program increased the trait of openness compared to the control group (Jackson, Hill, Payne, Roberts, & Stine-Morrow, 2012). The ability to train skills, change work environments, and create structure are all far easier to accomplish than moving attitudes.

With system thinking in place, individual attitudes stemming from entrenched dispositions may be difficult to modify but creating situations to trump dispositions have timelessly been successful. Providing the most inviting environment to welcome and persuade the desired attitudes should not be overlooked.

19 Five Project Manager Competencies

Competency modeling is a common way of assessing candidates and employees for selection, promotion, and training evaluation. Competencies are a listing of knowledge, skills, behaviors, and attitudes which are believed to be necessary for the employee to perform their job. An organization utilizes job analysis, organizational, group and individual performance measures and teams of subject matter experts to develop competencies that fit the culture of the organization. As important as the competency model for the positions, it is as essential to create behavior targets which to judge competency mastery against. These actions and results describe behavior and performance which identify poor, average, and excellent levels of competency. This paper will discuss five project manager competencies that are required in today's business climate based upon the descriptions of the duties, skills, and qualifications listed in the resource document entitled "PSY 838 Job Posting for Assignments."

Competing Values Framework

The competing values framework indicates eight managerial roles for developing strong managers including mentor, facilitator, monitor, coordinator, director, producer, broker, and innovator (Govender & Parumasur, 2010). Many of these roles are important for this job function however a few seem to apply more aptly. The ones that seem to meet the needs of the position are mentor in the area of coaching and counseling; coordinator, monitor, and director in terms of planning, reviewing and enforcing; and innovator in the role of system improver.

Project Manager Leadership Styles

Other general characteristics of effective project managers include styles similar to transformational, transactional and participative styles of leadership defined as intellectual, managerial, and emotional styles (Galvin, Gibbs, Sullivan, & Williams, 2014). It is typical for today's good managers to have flexibility in leadership style and be capable of applying multiple leadership dimensions as the situation requires (Galvin, Gibbs, Sullivan, & Williams, 2014). This position requires a balance of intelligence, analysis, and providing innovative recommendations. A fair amount of intellectual leadership is therefore warranted.

Managerial leadership traits are less obvious here. Managerial leadership proffers enthusiastic communication, advance planning, empowerment and development of others (Galvin, Gibbs, Sullivan, & Williams, 2014). Some of these traits are required such as planning and development of others but in a lesser sense enthusiastic communication and empowerment.

Emotional leadership provides for awareness, emotional strength, intuitiveness, sensitivity, and conscientiousness (Galvin, Gibbs, Sullivan, & Williams, 2014). It would seem that a human resources professional would be required to have this emotional sensitivity to human needs but the job posting mentions this not in the least. The position as stated is much more cut and dry, intellectual and managerial oriented. But should it be? I believe human resources should have this extra leadership competency dimension at its disposal.

Five Factors

Seeing that conscientiousness was a factor in emotional leadership brought this paper to looking at the Five Factor Model (FFM) and how it would apply to project manager competencies. The project manager is a member of a team. As such, team performance would be very important in the modern business climate. Research evaluating how personality impacts team performance indicates that Conscientiousness is often the most significant predictor (O'Neill & Allen, 2011). Each of the facets of Conscientiousness such as Organization and Achievement was positively and significantly predictive of team performance

(O'Neill & Allen, 2011). This aspect further underlines the fact that emotional leadership would be an important factor in the competencies of any leader working within a team environment.

Five Competencies

Five project manager competencies to nurture and develop or to put into the selection process of hiring a new project manager:

1) Mentor in the area of coaching and counseling
   a. Excellent - Co-creates ongoing employee development programs in accordance with company objectives, employee current KSAOs, and individual goals and objectives for all employees
   b. Average – Creates ongoing development programs with all mid-level management employees and above taking into account organizational goals and objectives
   c. Poor – Helps few key employees who seek out help

2) Intellectual leader and innovator in the role of system improvement
   a. Excellent – Provides analysis of recruiting efforts and creates new methods increasing selection effectiveness, reducing attrition by more than 30%
   b. Average – Solves problems with existing recruiting systems and keeps recruitment costs from rising
   c. Poor – Fails to address attrition issues and provides no real system improvements

3) Managerial leadership showing advanced advance planning and development of others
   a. Excellent - Reviews and addresses human resources issues, creates and implements employee incident reporting system

reducing company liability for lost time, reduce lost time by 30%

b. Average – Keeps reports and employee files up to date maintaining current system of operation, reduces lost time by 10%
c. Poor – Fails to address current lost time issues and does not reduce lost time

4) Emotional leadership, sensitivity to human needs
   a. Excellent - Develops personnel file for each employee and creates balanced life work program significantly increasing employee satisfaction on annual survey
   b. Average – Keeps current programs up to date, personally meets with each employee, continues transparent communication culture within organization
   c. Poor – Fails to keep up with satisfaction increasing programs and employee satisfaction significantly reduced within organization

5) Conscientiousness with achievement orientation
   a. Excellent – Achieves over 90% of goals set forth in position goals and objectives
   b. Average – Achieves over 70% of goals set forth in position goals and objectives
   c. Poor – Achieves less than 50% of goals set forth in position goals and objectives

The selection process should include structured assessment of the competencies developed through the job analysis. The same competencies are a basis for ongoing training and employee development.

20 Sales Performance Regression Analysis

This chapter will discuss a regression analysis of an existing sales employee workforce to determine a predictive model of sales performance. The analysis evaluates the connection between sales performance and extraversion, cognitive skills, and communication ability. Two applicants are to be chosen from a field of 10 applicants for two open positions. The question is what can be learned from the past performance of sales employees and can future selection be improved based upon this information.

A multiple regression analysis was conducted on figures from employees hired two years past. The resulting statistics are used to determine the two candidates that should be hired for the open positions.

Regression Procedure

The variables were entered into the IBM SPSS data analysis program using the stepwise procedure. Variables were added and removed until the best fit predictor equation model was found. The stepwise procedure selects variables to either keep or reject from the model in a successive manner (Qinggang, Koval, Mills, & Lee, 2008). The results of the stepwise procedure were modeled into a predictive equation after removing the variable Communication_Ability because of its non-significant benefit to the overall predictive nature:

Sales = (4710 x Extraversion) - (1765 x Cognitive_Skills) + 12999

Extraversion, Cognitive Skills, and Intercept explained a significant proportion of variance in Sales, adjusted $R^2 = .75$, $F(2, 9) = 14.65$, $p = .003$.

(See Table 2, Table 3, and Table 4)

Employee Performance and Coaching Needs

A number of employees are performing at various levels below their own predicted success and others below average. The mean sales of the group is $19,900 (Table 1). Unfortunately, the chart does not show or indicate if the sales are profitable sales.

$3784 is one standard deviation and anyone above $23,684 in sales is performing greater than one full standard deviation above the other employees. Only one employee is greater than one standard deviation above the mean. In fact, this one high performing employee is over two full standard deviations above the mean while 5 employees are below the group average. These below average performing employees also all suffer from the lowest Extraversion scores.

It becomes obvious that if Extraversion can be taught and increased by role play, teaching public speaking, and other training and development methods, then sales performance should vary accordingly. In a sales organization it becomes utmost important to understand the power of the initial impression. Initial expression is correlated with extraversion and helps form the present and future opinions of clients (Barrick, Dustin, Giluk, Stewart, Shaffer, & Swider, 2012). Training is recommended to be created for all sales employees focused on Extraversion.

Most Effective Principles of Consulting and Coaching

The most effective principles of consulting and coaching in this analysis would include job analysis, employee assessment, employee selection, and employee development. The ability to create selection tools would help the organization find its best candidates while focusing on economic utility. Validating selection is useful to minimize the risk in selecting new employees. Consulting and coaching can be used to uncover, validate, develop, and expand on organizational expectations aligned with company, team, and individual goals (Čiutienė & Petrauskas, 2012).

New Employee Selection

As discussed previously the prediction equation for Sales is:
Sales = (4710 x Extraversion) - (1765 x Cognitive_Skills) + 12999

Extraversion, Cognitive_Skills, and Intercept explained a significant proportion of variance in Sales, adjusted $R^2 = .75$, $F(2, 9) = 14.65$, $p = .003$.

Substituting into the equation the trait scores of each of the candidates will yield predicted best ranked candidates of Jane Doe, and Burt McIntyre. These would be the two candidates that would have the highest predicted performance based on the target criteria of Sales as shown in Table 2. All tables and data (in tables 1 through 5) appear on the following pages.

Using data to link performance with assessments such as personality traits and cognitive skills may provide hiring and training opportunities. The more focus is placed on job analysis, key performance indicators, and assessment, the more likely the system may be modified to acquire, train, and retain employees with the best fit and most likely potential for success and happiness in each position.

Table 1: Descriptive Statistics

Descriptive Statistics

	N	Minimum	Maximum	Mean	Std. Deviation	Variance	Skewness		Kurtosis	
	Statistic	Statistic	Statistic	Statistic	Statistic	Statistic	Statistic	Std. Error	Statistic	Std. Error
Sales	10	15000	28000	19900.00	3784.471	14322222.222	.881	.687	1.235	1.334
Valid N (listwise)	10									

Table 2: Sales Figures Predicted

Applicant	Extraversion	Cognitive Skills	Communication Ability	Predicted Sales
John Smith	5	9	17	20664
Jane Doe	4	6	11	21249
Burt McIntyre	7	13	19	23024
Elizabeth Reddin	3	5	7	18304
James Golstein	6	12	15	20079
Shawn George	4	10	7	14189
Susan Williams	3	6	8	16539
Jose Valencia	5	10	12	18899
Levi Ogletree	6	14	20	16549
Pat Sylvester	2	8	6	8299

Table 3

Model Summary

Model	R	R Square	Adjusted R Square	Std. Error of the Estimate	Change Statistics				
					R Square Change	F Change	df1	df2	Sig. F Change
1	.696[a]	.485	.420	2881.052	.485	7.529	1	8	.025
2	.898[b]	.807	.752	1884.460	.322	11.699	1	7	.011

a. Predictors: (Constant), Extraversion

b. Predictors: (Constant), Extraversion, Cognitive Skills

Table 4

ANOVA[a]

Model		Sum of Squares	df	Mean Square	F	Sig.
1	Regression	62496330.275	1	62496330.275	7.529	.025[b]
	Residual	66403669.725	8	8300458.716		
	Total	128900000.000	9			
2	Regression	104041678.129	2	52020839.065	14.649	.003[c]
	Residual	24858321.871	7	3551188.839		
	Total	128900000.000	9			

a. Dependent Variable: Sales

b. Predictors: (Constant), Extraversion

c. Predictors: (Constant), Extraversion, Cognitive Skills

Table 5

Coefficients

Model		Unstandardized Coefficients		Standardized Coefficients	t	Sig.
		B	Std. Error	Beta		
1	(Constant)	7688.073	4542.788		1.692	.129
	Extraversion	2394.495	872.645	.696	2.744	.025
2	(Constant)	12998.624	3352.571		3.877	.006
	Extraversion	4709.766	885.436	1.370	5.319	.001
	Cognitive Skills	-1764.787	515.962	-.881	-3.420	.011

a. Dependent Variable: Sales

21 Ethical Competency Testing Practices

Psychological and competency testing are ethical practices during the selection process as long as they have high validity and reliability in predicting performance as well as are not used in a biased manner or contribute to disparate treatment or impact of protected groups.

The problem of using psychological and competency testing has been through misapplication by unqualified facilitators rather than what was in the tests themselves (Moreland, Eyde, Robertson, Primoff, & Most, 1995). The trouble may stem from not understanding applicable measurement methodology, misapplying results, and inability to interpret testing outcomes (Moreland, Eyde, Robertson, Primoff, & Most, 1995).

The number of people without backgrounds in assessments testing or an understanding of how to use the scores are increasing (Taylor, 2009). The amount of testing that is occurring, the number of tests available, and the required knowledge of validity, ethics, and standards are growing (Taylor, 2009).

Criterion-related validity of the assessment must be a predictor of job performance in personnel selection (Arthur, Bell, Villado, & Doverspike, 2006). Good and relevant tests should be used at the right time and applied in a knowledgeable manner while taking into consideration the needs, culture, and unique situations of the people being tested (Bartram, 2001).

The most effective strategies for avoiding invasion of privacy, breaches of confidentiality, and future ethical issues when using psychological and competency testing is to first utilize trained professionals in selection, administration, and interpretation of test results. There needs to be a promise of confidentiality when a company administers psychological tests (Eberlein, 1980). The Supreme Court has ruled that there is an amount of confidentiality that is needed to protect the candidate and guard the integrity of the psychological test (Eberlein, 1980).

Results of testing must not be shared, and questions should not be asked that delve into protected status of candidates. Only job and task related questions should be asked in terms of competency and questions must contain valid and reliable measures which predict performance if personality or psychological tests are administered.

Workplace Assessment Summary

There are several items that pique interest and contour thoughts on workplace assessment. Structured interviews, skill assessment, general mental ability, and personality testing all work together to give a better overview of candidates in the selection process as well as give the basis for valid and reliable measures with which to compare candidates.

The structured interview based upon job analysis and job tasks has now become a tool to use within many companies. Yet, many small companies rely upon a more casual interview which only gives a cursory feeling based upon initial impression about candidates. It is not enough. Companies typically assess fit with the organization, but most do not base selection on psychological testing. It is recommended to research the use of personality testing in the future to help find fit and predict and compare future performance of candidates.

It is important to accurately measure or ascertain the level of knowledge, skills, and abilities of candidates to make wiser decisions in the selection process. Studies have indicated that job knowledge is of greater importance than general mental ability in prediction of job performance (Stauffer, 2010). You may have heard the expression, "there is no substitute for experience."

General mental ability is also a big plus. A common theme of the Society of Industrial and Organizational Psychology (SIOP) is that cognitive aptitude assessments should always be conducted when personnel are being selected (Murphy, Cronin, & Tam, 2003). As with all the preceding, adverse impact needs to be monitored and fair hiring methods must be used that are in keeping with Equal Employment Opportunity law and other legal requirements against discrimination in the work place.

22 E^6 Excellence

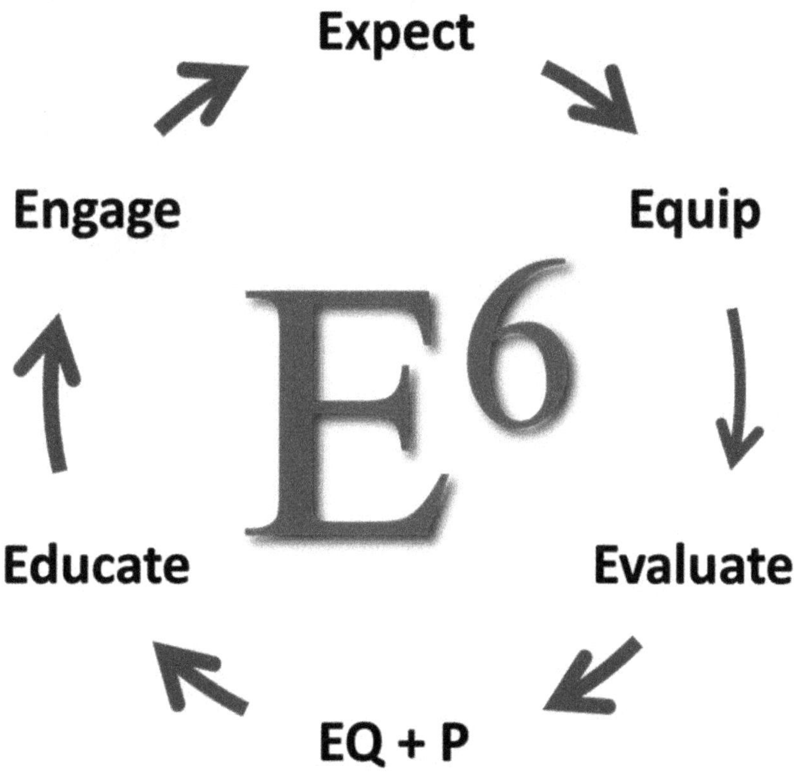

Expect

Mission/Vision:

Culture:

Goals:

Clearly communicated, visual, and omnipresent.

Memory tip:

Equip

Machinery, materials, and tools:

Processes and procedures:

Environment, PPE, and uniform:

SOP, maintenance, quality, visual

Memory tip:

Evaluate

Job analysis:

Key performance indicators:

Knowledge, skills, and abilities:

Training program content and effectiveness-assessment:

Memory tip:

Emotional Intelligence and Personality

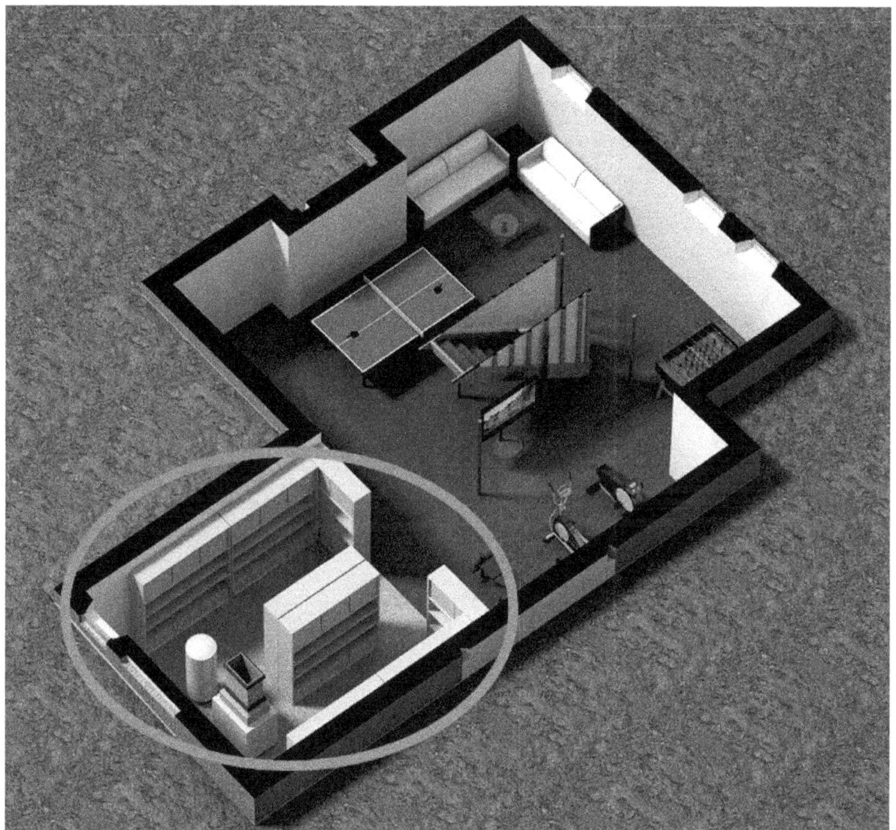

Emotional Intelligence:

Personality traits:

Innate strengths:

Education

Individual development program:

Skill and knowledge-based job training:

Cultural elements and expectations:

Co-create, individual, team, company

Memory tip:

Engage

Psychosocial and team work:

Feedback and 360 interviews:

Rewards, benefits, and life balance:

Emotions, satisfaction, inclusion, and greater good

Memory tip:

23 Faces of Emotion

Clockwise from top left, happy, sad, contempt, surprise, anger, disgust, and fear

References

Bocchiaro, P., & Zimbardo, P. G. (2010). Defying Unjust Authority: An Exploratory Study. Current Psychology, 29(2), 155-170. doi:10.1007/s12144-010-9080-z http://library.gcu.edu:2048/login?url=http://search.ebscohost.com/login.aspx?direct=true&db=a9h&AN=50329170&site=eds-live&scope=site

Navarick, D. J. (2012). Historical Psychology and the Milgram Paradigm: Tests of an Experimentally Derived Model of Defiance Using Accounts of Massacres by Nazi Reserve Police Battalion 101. Psychological Record, 62(1), 133-154. http://library.gcu.edu:2048/login?url=http://search.ebscohost.com/login.aspx?direct=true&db=eric&AN=EJ987171&site=ehost-live&scope=site

Navarick, D. J. (2009). Reviving the Milgram Obedience Paradigm in the Era of Informed Consent. Psychological Record, 59(2), 155-170. http://library.gcu.edu:2048/login?url=http://search.ebscohost.com/login.aspx?direct=true&db=eric&AN=EJ838374&site=ehost-live&scope=site

Reicher, S., & Haslam, S. (2011). After shock? Towards a social identity explanation of the Milgram 'obedience' studies. British Journal Of Social Psychology, 50(1), 163-169. doi:10.1111/j.2044-8309.2010.02015.x http://library.gcu.edu:2048/login?url=http://search.ebscohost.com/login.aspx?direct=true&db=a9h&AN=64995520&site=eds-live&scope=site

Russell, N. (2011). Milgram's obedience to authority experiments: Origins and early evolution. British Journal Of Social Psychology, 50(1), 140-162. doi:10.1348/014466610X492205. http://library.gcu.edu:2048/login?url=http://search.ebscohost.c

om/login.aspx?direct=true&db=a9h&AN=64995527&site=eds-live&scope=site

Bonebright, D. A. (2010). 40 years of storming: a historical review of Tuckman's model of small group development. *Human Resource Development International, 13*(1), 111-120. doi:10.1080/13678861003589099

Bouckenooghe, D., Devos, G., & Van den Broeck, H. (2009). Organizational change questionnaire–climate of change, processes, and readiness: Development of a new instrument. *Journal Of Psychology, 143*(6), 559-599. Retrieved from http://library.gcu.edu:2048/login?url=http://search.ebscohost.com/login.aspx?direct=true&db=bth&AN=44867977&site=eds-live&scope=site

Drack, M. (2009). Ludwig von Bertalanffy's early system approach. *Systems Research & Behavioral Science, 26*(5), 563-572. doi:10.1002/sres.992

Aviezer, H., Hassin, R. R., Ryan, J., Grady, C., Susskind, J., Anderson, A., & ... Bentin, S. (2008). Angry, disgusted, or afraid? Studies on the malleability of emotion perception. Psychological Science (Wiley-Blackwell), 19(7), 724-732. doi:10.1111/j.1467-9280.2008.02148.x

Azogu, I., de la Tremblaye, P. B., Dunbar, M., Lebreton, M., LeMarec, N., & Plamondon, H. (2015). Acute sleep deprivation enhances avoidance learning and spatial memory and induces delayed alterations in neurochemical expression of GR, TH, DRD1, pCREB and Ki67 in rats. Behavioural Brain Research, 279177-190. doi:10.1016/j.bbr.2014.11.015

Belhekar, M. N., Bhalerao, S. S., & Munshi, R. P. (2014). Ethics reporting practices in clinical research publications: A review of four Indian journals. Perspectives In Clinical Research, 5(3), 129-133. doi:10.4103/2229-3485.134316

Bishop S. J., Jenkins R., Lawrence A. D. (2007). Neural processing of fearful faces: effects of anxiety are gated by perceptual capacity limitations. Cereb. Cortex 17, 1595–1603. doi:10.1093/cercor/bhl070

Bordens, K. S., & Abbott, B. B. (2008). Research design and methods: A process approach (7th ed.). Boston, MA: McGraw Hill.

Brace, N., Kemp, R., & Snelgar, R. (2006). SPSS for psychologists (3rd ed.). Mahwah, NJ: Lawrence Erlbaum Associates, Publisher.

Canli T., Sivers H., Whitfiled S. L., Gotlib I. H., Gabrieli J. D. E. (2002). Amygdala response to happy faces as a function of extraversion. Science 295, 2191. doi:10.1126/science.1068749

Chen, J. (2014). Face recognition as a predictor of social cognitive ability: Effects of emotion and race on face processing. Asian Journal of Social Psychology 17, 61-69. doi:10.1111/ajsp.12041

DeYoung (2006). Higher-order factors of the Big Five in a multi-informant sample. Journal of Personality and Social Psychology.

Demirbuga, S., Sahin, E., Ozver, I., Aliustaoglu, S., Kandemir, E., Varkal, M., Ince, H. (2012). Facial emotion recognition in patients with violent schizophrenia. Schizophrenia Research, 144, 142-145. doi:10.1016/j.schres.2012.12.015

Diehl-Schmid, J., Pohl, C., Ruprecht, C., Wagenpfeil, S., Foerstl, H., & Kurz, A. (2007). The Ekman 60 Faces Test as a diagnostic instrument in frontotemporal dementia. Archives of Clinical Neuropsychology, 22, 459-464. doi:10.1016/j.acn.2007.01.024

Digman, J.M. (1990). Personality structure: Emergence of the five-factor model. Annual Review of Psychology 41, 417–440. doi:10.1146/annurev.ps.41.020190.002221

Dimitrov, D. M. (2008). Quantitative research in education. New York, NY: Whittier

Publications Inc.

Dodich, A., Cerami, C., Canessa, N., Crespi, C., Marcone, A., Arpone, M., ... & Cappa, S. F. (2014). Emotion recognition from facial expressions: a normative study of the Ekman 60-Faces Test in the Italian population. Neurological Sciences, 35(7), 1015-1021.

Ekman, P., Friesen, W. V. (1971). Constants across cultures in the face and emotion. Journal Of Personality And Social Psychology, 17(2), 124-129. doi:10.1037/h0030377

Emmerling, R. J., & Goleman, D. (2003). Emotional Intelligence: Issues and common misunderstandings. Retrieved from http://www.eiconsortium.org/pdf/EI_Issues_And_Common_Misunderstandings.pdf

Ewbank M. P., Fox E., Calder A. J. (2010). The interaction between gaze and facial expression in the amygdala and extended amygdala is modulated by anxiety. Front. Hum. Neurosci. 4, 56. doi:10.3389/fnhum.2010.00056

Faul, F., Erdfelder, E., Buchner, A., & Lang, A. G. (2014). G*Power Version 3.1.9 [computer software]. Uiversität Kiel, Germany. Retrieved from http://www.gpower.hhu.de/en/html

Few, L. R., Miller, J. D., Morse, J. Q., Yaggi, K. E., Reynolds, S. K., & Pilkonis, P. A. (2010). Examining the reliability and validity of clinician ratings on the five-factor model score sheet. PubMed Central, 17(4), 440–453. doi:10.1177/1073191110372210

Furnham, A. F. (1997). Knowing and faking one's five-factor personality score.Journal of Personality Assessment, 69(1), 229-243.

Gall, M. D., Gall, J. P., & Borg, W. R. (2007). Educational research: An introduction.(8 th edition). Boston : Pearson/Allyn & Bacon . Hewitt, J. & Peters, V. (2006). Using wikis to support knowledge building in a graduate education course. In E. Pearson & P. Bohman (Eds.), Proceedings of World Conference on Educational Multimedia, Hypermedia and

Telecommunications 2006 (pp. 2200-2204). Chesapeake, VA: AACE

Gendron, M., Roberson, D., van der Vyver, J., & Barrett, L. (2014). Perceptions of emotion from facial expressions are not culturally universal: Evidence from a remote culture. Emotion, 14(2), 251-262. doi:10.1037/a0036052

George, D. & Mallery, P. (2010). SPSS for Windows step by step: a simple guide and reference, 18.0 update (11th ed.). Boston, MA: Allyn and Bacon.

Guido, G., Pino, G., & Frangipane, D. (2011). The role of credibility and perceived image of supermarket stores as valuable providers of over-the-counter drugs. Journal Of Marketing Management, 27(3/4), 207-224. doi:10.1080/0267257X.2011.545669

Howell, D. C. (2010). Statistical methods for psychology (7th ed.). Belmont CA: Wadsworth Cengage Learning.

John, O. P., & Srivastava, S. (1999). The Big-Five trait taxonomy: History, measurement, and

theoretical perspectives. In L. A. Pervin & O. P. John (Eds.), Handbook of personality: Theory and research (Vol. 2, pp. 102–138). New York: Guilford Press.

Kayyal, M. H., & Russell, J. A. (2013). Americans and Palestinians judge spontaneous facial expressions of emotion. Emotion, 13(5), 891-904. doi:10.1037/a0033244

Körner, A., Czajkowska, Z., Albani, C., Drapeau, M., Geyer, M., & Braehler, E. (2015). Efficient and valid assessment of personality traits: population norms of a brief version of the NEO Five-Factor Inventory (NEO-FFI). Archives Of Psychiatry & Psychotherapy, 17(1), 21-32. doi:10.12740/APP/36086

Künecke, J., Hildebrandt, A., Recio, G., Sommer, W., & Wilhelm, O. (2014). Facial EMG Responses to Emotional Expressions Are Related to Emotion Perception Ability. Plos ONE, 9(1), 1-10. doi:10.1371/journal.pone.0084053

Matsumoto, D., & Ekman, P. (1988). Japanese and Caucasian facial expressions of emotion
(JACFEE) [Slides]. San Francisco, CA: Intercultural and Emotion Research Laboratory, Departmentof Psychology, San Francisco State University.

McCrae RR, Zonderman AB, Costa PT, Jr, Bond MH, Paunonen SV (1996). Evaluating replicability of factors in the Revised NEO Personality Inventory: Confirmatory factor analysis versus Procrustes rotation. Journal of Personality and Social Psychology.

Meyers, L. S., Gamst, G., & Guarino, A. J. (2013). Applied multivariate research: Design and interpretation (2nd ed.). Thousand Oaks, CA: Sage. [PDF]. Retrieved from http://gcumedia.com/digital-resources/sage/2013/applied-multivariate-research_design-and-interpretation_ebook_2e.php

Mobbs, D., Weiskopf, N., Lau, H., Featherstone, E., Dolan, R., & Frith, C. (2006). The Kuleshov effect: the influence of contextual framing on emotional attributions. Social Cognitive And Affective Neuroscience, 1(2), 95-106. Retrieved from http://library.gcu.edu:2048/login?url=http://search.ebscohost.com/login.aspx?direct=true&db=a9h&AN=45280012&site=eds-live&scope=site

Neumann, R., Schulz, S., Lozo, L., & Alpers, G. (2014). Automatic facial responses to near-threshold presented facial displays of emotion: Imitation or evaluation? Biological Psychology, 96, 144-149. doi:10.1016/j.biopsycho.2013.12.009

Nowicki, S. Jr., & Hartigan, M. (2001). Accuracy of facial affect recognition as a function of locus of control orientation and anticipated interpersonal interaction. The Journal of Social Psychology, 128(3), 363–372. doi: 10.1080/00224545.1988.9713753

Pagano, R. R. (2009). Understanding statistics in the behavioral sciences (9th ed.). Belmont CA: Wadsworth Cengage Learning.

Powledge, T. T. (2011). Behavioral epigenetics: How nurture shapes nature. Bioscience, 61(8), 588-592. Retrieved from http://library.gcu.edu:2048/login?url=http://search.ebscohost.com.library.gcu.edu:2048/login.aspx?direct=true&db=ofs&AN=64118089&site=eds-live&scope=site

Proverbio, A., Calbi, M., Manfredi, M., & Zani, A. (2014). Comprehending body language and mimics: an ERP and neuroimaging study on Italian actors and viewers. Plos ONE, 9(3), 1-15. doi:10.1371/journal.pone.0091294

Recio, G., Schacht, A., & Sommer, W. (2014). Recognizing dynamic facial expressions of emotion: Specificity and intensity effects in event-related brain potentials. Biological Psychology, 96111-125. doi:10.1016/j.biopsycho.2013.12.003

Rossa, K. R., Smith, S. S., Allan, A. C., & Sullivan, K. A. (2014). Original article: the effects of sleep restriction on executive inhibitory control and affect in young adults. Journal Of Adolescent Health, 55287-292. doi:10.1016/j.jadohealth.2013.12.034

Royse, D., Thyer, B. A., & Padgett, D. K. (2010). Program evaluation: An introduction (5th ed.). Belmont, CA: Cengage Learning.

Sackett, P. R, Walmsley, P. T. (2014). Which personality attributes are most important in the workplace? Perspectives on Psychological Science, 9(5), 538-551. doi:10.1177/1745691614543972

Sassenrath, C., Sassenberg, K., Ray, D. G., Scheiter, K., & Jarodzka, H. (2014). A motivational determinant of facial emotion recognition: Regulatory focus affects recognition of emotions in faces. Plos ONE, 9(11), 1-9. doi:10.1371/journal.pone.0112383.

Srivastava, S. (2015). Measuring the Big Five Personality Factors. Retrieved September 23, 2015 from http://psdlab.uoregon.edu/bigfive.html

Stevens, J. P. (2009). Applied multivariate statistics for the social sciences (5th ed.). Mahwah, NJ: Routledge Academic.

Tabachnick, B. G. & Fidell, L. S. (2012). Using multivariate statistics (6th ed.). Boston, MA: Pearson.

Vecchione, M., Dentale, F., Alessandri, G., & Barbaranelli, C. (2014). Fakability of Implicit and Explicit Measures of the Big Five: Research findings from organizational settings. International Journal of Selection and Assessment,22(2), 211-218.

Wang, B. (2013). Gender difference in recognition memory for neutral and emotional faces. Memory, 21(8), 991-1003. doi:10.1080/09658211.2013.771273

Wilhelm, O., Hildebrandt, A., Manske, K., Schacht, A., Sommer, W., Walla, P., & Korb, S. (2014). Test battery for measuring the perception and recognition of facial expressions of emotion. Frontiers In Psychology, 51-23. doi:10.3389/fpsyg.2014.00404

Wranik, T., Barrett, L. F., & Salovey, P. (2007). Intelligent emotion regulation. In Handbook of emotion regulation, 393-428.

Bonebright, D. A. (2010). 40 years of storming: a historical review of Tuckman's model of small group development. Human Resource Development International, 13(1), 111-120. doi:10.1080/13678861003589099

Bouckenooghe, D., Devos, G., & Van den Broeck, H. (2009). Organizational change questionnaire–climate of change, processes, and readiness: Development of a new instrument. Journal Of Psychology, 143(6), 559-599. Retrieved from http://library.gcu.edu:2048/login?url=http://search.ebscohost.com/login.aspx?direct=true&db=bth&AN=44867977&site=eds-live&scope=site

Drack, M. (2009). Ludwig von Bertalanffy's early system approach. Systems Research & Behavioral Science, 26(5), 563-572. doi:10.1002/sres.992

Du, S., Swaen, V., Lindgreen, A., & Sen, S. (2013). The Roles of Leadership Styles in Corporate Social Responsibility. Journal Of Business Ethics, 114(1), 155-169. doi:10.1007/s10551-012-1333-3

Fuqua, D., & Newman, J., (2002). The role of systems theory in consulting psychology, in Lowman, Rodney, L., The California school of organization studies handbook of organizational consulting psychology: A comprehensive guide to theory, skills, and techniques. (pp. 76-105). San Francisco, CA: Jossy-Bass.

George, L. G., Helson, R., & John, O. P. (2011). The "CEO" of women's work lives: How Big Five Conscientiousness, Extraversion, and Openness predict 50 years of work experiences in a changing sociocultural context. Journal Of Personality And Social Psychology, 101(4), 812-830. doi:10.1037/a0024290

Lowman, L. L. (2002). The California school of organization studies hand book of organizational consulting psychology: A comprehensive guide to theory, skills, and techniques. San Francisco, CA: Jossey-Bass.

Onishi, A. (2005). A Teacher: The Power of Teaching Students about Their Strengths. Educational Horizons, 83(3), 206-209. Retrieved from http://library.gcu.edu:2048/login?url=http://search.ebscohost.com/login.aspx?direct=true&db=ofs&AN=507984759&site=eds-live&scope=site

Powell, S. (2011). Wayside Teaching: Building Autonomy. Middle School Journal, 43(2), 38-40. Retrieved from http://library.gcu.edu:2048/login?url=http://search.ebscohost.com/login.aspx?direct=true&db=eric&AN=EJ961650&site=ehost-live&scope=site

Segers, J., Vloeberghs, D., Henderickx, E., & Inceoglu, I. (2011). Structuring and understanding the coaching industry: The coaching cube. Academy Of Management Learning & Education, 10(2), 204-221. doi:10.5465/AMLE.2011.62798930

Xiaobei, L., Frenkel, S. J., & Sanders, K. (2011). Strategic HRM as process: how HR system and organizational climate strength influence Chinese employee attitudes. International Journal Of Human Resource Management, 22(9), 1825-1842. doi:10.1080/09585192.2011.573965

Barrick, M. R., Mount, M. K., & Li, N. (2013). The theory of purposeful work behavior: the role of personality, higher-order goals, and job characteristics. Academy Of Management Review, 38(1), 132-153. doi:10.5465/amr.2010.0479

Zoer, I., de Graaf, L., Kuijer, P. M., Prinzie, P., Hoozemans, M. M., & Frings-Dresen, M. W. (2012). Matching work capacities and demands at job placement in employees with disabilities. Work, 42(2), 205-214.

Leidner, D., Koch, H., & Gonzalez, E. (2010). Assimilating generation y IT new hires into USAA's workforce: The role of an enterprise 2.0 system. MIS Quarterly Executive, 9(4), 229-242. Retrieved from http://library.gcu.edu:2048/login?url=http://search.ebscohost.com.library.gcu.edu:2048/login.aspx?direct=true&db=bth&AN=58657250&site=eds-live&scope=site

Haliru, B., & Kabir, B. (2011). Mentorship as a tool for human resources: Local government experience. IFE Psychologia, 104-111. Retrieved from http://library.gcu.edu:2048/login?url=http://search.ebscohost.com.library.gcu.edu:2048/login.aspx?direct=true&db=a9h&AN=66960296&site=eds-live&scope=site

Ghorbanhosseini, M. (2013). The effect of organizational culture, teamwork and organizational development on organizational commitment: the mediating role of human capital. Tehnicki Vjesnik / Technical Gazette, 20(6), 1019-1025. Retrieved from http://library.gcu.edu:2048/login?url=http://search.ebscohost.com.library.gcu.edu:2048/login.aspx?direct=true&db=a9h&AN=93360282&site=eds-live&scope=site

Li, W., Fay, D., Frese, M., Harms, P. D., & Gao, X. (2014). Reciprocal relationship between proactive personality and work characteristics: A latent change score approach. Journal Of Applied Psychology, doi:10.1037/a0036169

Prabhu, V. P. (2013). Proactive personality and intent to remain with an organization: Understanding factors affecting retention of israeli employees. Journal Of Management Policy & Practice, 14(4), 11-25. Retrieved from http://library.gcu.edu:2048/login?url=http://search.ebscohost.com/login.aspx?direct=true&db=bth&AN=94484552&site=eds-live&scope=site

Crant, J. J., Kim, T., & Wang, J. (2011). Dispositional antecedents of demonstration and usefulness of voice behavior. Journal Of Business & Psychology, 26(3), 285-297. doi:10.1007/s10869-010-9197-y

Rodrigues, N., & Rebelo, T. (2013). Incremental validity of proactive personality over the Big Five for predicting job performance of software engineers in an innovative context. Journal of Work and Organizational Psychology, 29(1), 21-27. doi:10.5093/tr2013a4

Jackson, J. J., Hill, P. L., Payne, B. R., Roberts, B. W., & Stine-Morrow, E. L. (2012). Can an old dog learn (and want to experience) new tricks? Cognitive training increases openness to experience in older adults. Psychology And Aging, 27(2), 286-292. doi:10.1037/a0025918

Galvin, T., Gibbs, M., Sullivan, J., & Williams, C. (2014). Leadership Competencies of Project Managers: An Empirical Study of Emotional, Intellectual, and Managerial Dimensions. Journal Of Economic Development, Management, IT, Finance &

Marketing, 6(1), 35-60. Retrieved from http://library.gcu.edu:2048/login?url=http://search.ebscohost.com/login.aspx?direct=true&db=bth&AN=94191261&site=eds-live&scope=site

Govender, P., & Parumasur, S. B. (2010). Evaluating the roles and competencies that are critical considerations for management development. SAJIP: South African Journal Of Industrial Psychology, 36(1), 1-11. doi:10.4102/sajip v36i1.835

O'Neill, T. A., & Allen, N. J. (2011). Personality and the prediction of team performance. European Journal Of Personality, 25(1), 31-42. doi:10.1002/per.769

Muckle, T. J., Plaus, K. A., Henderson, J., & Waters, E. (2012). Professional Practice Analysis: Determining Job Relatedness of the Certification Examination for Nurse Anesthetists. Journal Of Nursing Regulation, 3(3), 55. Retrieved from http://library.gcu.edu:2048/login?url=http://search.ebscohost.com/login.aspx?direct=true&db=edb&AN=82382073&site=eds-live&scope=site

Čiutienė, R., & Petrauskas, P. (2012). Management by objectives using coaching. Economics & Management, 17(4), 1559-1563. doi:10.5755/j01.em.17.4.3029

Qinggang, W., Koval, J. J., Mills, C. A., & Lee, K. (2008). Determination of the selection statistics and best significance level in backward stepwise logistic regression. Communications In Statistics: Simulation & Computation, 37(1), 62-72. doi:10.1080/03610910701723625

Clarke, C., Harcourt, M., & Flynn, M. (2013). Clinical governance, performance appraisal and interactional and procedural fairness at a New Zealand public hospital. Journal Of Business Ethics, 117(3), 667-678. doi:10.1007/s10551-012-1550-9

Martin, D., Bartol, K., & Kehoe, P. (2000). The legal ramifications of performance appraisal: the growing significance. Public

Personnel Management, 29(3), 379-405. Retrieved from http://library.gcu.edu:2048/login?url=http://search.ebscohost.com.library.gcu.edu:2048/login.aspx?direct=true&db=ccm&AN=2001013066&site=eds-live&scope=site

Werner, J. M., & Bolino, M. C. (1997). Explaining u.s. courts of appeals decisions involving performance appraisal: accuracy, fairness, and validation. Personnel Psychology, 50(1), 1-24. Retrieved from http://library.gcu.edu:2048/login?url=http://search.ebscohost.com.library.gcu.edu:2048/login.aspx?direct=true&db=bth&AN=9703303251&site=ehost-live&scope=site

Saks, A. M., & Burke, L. A. (2012). An investigation into the relationship between training evaluation and the transfer of training. International Journal Of Training And Development, 16(2), 118-127. Retrieved from http://library.gcu.edu:2048/login?url=http://search.ebscohost.com.library.gcu.edu:2048/login.aspx?direct=true&db=eric&AN=EJ964490&site=eds-live&scope=site

Alliger, G. M., & Janak, E. A. (1989). Kirkpatrick's levels of training criteria: thirty years later. Personnel Psychology, 42(2), 331-342. Retrieved from http://library.gcu.edu:2048/login?url=http://search.ebscohost.com/login.aspx?direct=true&db=bth&AN=6258872&site=eds-live&scope=site

Iqbal, M., & Khan, R. (2011). The growing concept and uses of training needs assessment: A review with proposed model. Journal Of European Industrial Training, 35(5), 439-466. doi:10.1108/03090591111138017

van Eerde, W. W., Tang, K., & Talbot, G. (2008). The mediating role of training utility in the relationship between training needs assessment and organizational effectiveness. International

Journal Of Human Resource Management, 19(1), 63-73. doi:10.1080/09585190701763917

Crow, R. (1996). You cannot improve my performance by measuring it!. Journal For Quality & Participation, 19(1), 62. Retrieved from http://library.gcu.edu:2048/login?url=http://search.ebscohost.com/login.aspx?direct=true&db=ofs&AN=9602264292&site=eds-live&scope=site

Aluri, R., & Reichel, M. (1994). Performance evaluation: A deadly disease?. Journal Of Academic Librarianship, 20(3), 145. Retrieved from http://library.gcu.edu:2048/login?url=http://search.ebscohost.com/login.aspx?direct=true&db=a9h&AN=9408240891&site=eds-live&scope=site

David, B. (2012). The legal concept of corporate responsibility. Contemporary Readings In Law & Social Justice, 4(2), 330-335. Retrieved from http://library.gcu.edu:2048/login?url=http://search.ebscohost.com.library.gcu.edu:2048/login.aspx?direct=true&db=a9h&AN=85777562&site=eds-live&scope=site

Moreland, K. L., Eyde, L. D., Robertson, G. J., Primoff, E. S., & Most, R. B. (1995). Assessment of test user qualifications: A research-based measurement procedure. American Psychologist, 50(1), 14-23. doi:10.1037/0003-066X.50.1.14

Bartram, D. (2001). Guidelines for test users: A review of national and international initiatives. European Journal Of Psychological Assessment, 17(3), 173-186. doi:10.1027//1015-5759.17.3.173

Taylor, L. (2009). Developing assessment literacy. Annual Review Of Applied Linguistics, 29(1), 21-36. doi:10.1017/S0267190509090035

Arthur, W. r., Bell, S. T., Villado, A. J., & Doverspike, D. (2006). The use of person-organization fit in employment decision making:

An assessment of its criterion-related validity. Journal Of Applied Psychology, 91(4), 786-801. doi:10.1037/0021-9010.91.4.786

Eberlein, L. (1980). Confidentiality of industrial psychological tests. Professional Psychology, 11(5), 749-754. doi:10.1037/0735-7028.11.5.749

Stauffer, J. (2010). A basis for asserting the efficacy of alternative abilities in personnel selection. Business Studies Journal, 265-81. Retrieved from http://library.gcu.edu:2048/login?url=http://search.ebscohost.com/login.aspx?direct=true&db=bth&AN=67195140&site=eds-live&scope=site

Murphy, K. R., Cronin, B. E., & Tam, A. P. (2003). Controversy and consensus regarding the use of cognitive ability testing in organizations. Journal Of Applied Psychology, 88(4), 660-671. doi:10.1037/0021-9010.88.4.660

Zhang, J., Li, Y., & Wu, C. (2013). The influence of individual and team cognitive ability on operators' task and safety performance: A multilevel field study in nuclear power plants. Plos ONE, 8(12), 1-9. doi:10.1371/journal.pone.0084528

Hunter, J.E., & Schmidt, F.L. (1998). The validity and utility of selection methods in personnel psychology: practical and theoretical implications of 85 years of research findings. Psychological Bulletin, 124(2), 262-274. Retrieved from http://mavweb.mnsu.edu/howard/Schmidt%20and%20Hunter%201998%20Validity%20and%20Utility%20Psychological%20Bulletin.pdf

Tews, M. J., Michel, J. W., & Lyons, B. D. (2010). Beyond personality: the impact of GMA on performance for entry-level service employees. Journal Of Service Management, 21(3), 344-362. doi:10.1108/09564231011050797

Vasalampi, K., Parker, P., Tolvanen, A., Lüdtke, O., Salmela-Aro, K., & Trautwein, U. (2014). Integration of personality constructs: The role of traits and motivation in the willingness to exert effort in academic and social life domains. Journal Of Research In Personality, 4898-106. doi:10.1016/j.jrp.2013.11.004

Van Iddekinge, C. H., Raymark, P. H., & Eidson, J. E. (2011). An examination of the validity and incremental value of needed-at-entry ratings for a customer service job. Applied Psychology: An International Review, 60(1), 24-45. doi:10.1111/j.1464-0597.2010.00425.x

Mount, M. K., Oh, I., & Burns, M. (2008). Incremental validity of perceptual speed and accuracy over general mental ability. Personnel Psychology, 61(1), 113-139. doi:10.1111/j.1744-6570.2008.00107.x

Birkeland, S. A., Manson, T. M., Kisamore, J. L., Brannick, M. T., & Smith, M. A. (2006). A meta-analytic investigation of job applicant faking on personality measures. International Journal Of Selection & Assessment, 14(4), 317-335. doi:10.1111/j.1468-2389.2006.00354.x

Galić, Z., & Jerneić, Ž. (2013). Measuring faking on five-factor personality questionnaires: the usefulness of communal and agentic management scales. Journal Of Personnel Psychology, 12(3), 115-123. doi:10.1027/1866-5888/a000087

Inslegers, R., Vanheule, S., Meganck, R., Debaere, V., Trenson, E., Desmet, M., & Roelstraete, B. (2012). The assessment of the social cognition and object relations scale on TAT and interview data. Journal Of Personality Assessment, 94(4), 372-379. doi:10.1080/00223891.2012.662187

Gruber, N., & Kreuzpointner, L. (2013). Measuring the reliability of picture story exercises like the TAT. Plos ONE, 8(11), 1. doi:10.1371/journal.pone.0079450

Wille, B., De Fruyt, F., & Feys, M. (2013). Big five traits and intrinsic success in the new career era: a 15-year longitudinal study on employability and work-family conflict. Applied Psychology: An International Review, 62(1), 124-156. doi:10.1111/j.1464-0597.2012.00516.x

Hernandez, J. S. (2012). Tips for recruiting and retaining the best physicians. Physician Executive, 38(6), 64-67. Retrieved from http://library.gcu.edu:2048/login?url=http://search.ebscohost.com/login.aspx?direct=true&db=bth&AN=83751536&site=eds-live&scope=site

Falcone, P. (1996). 96 Great interview questions to ask before you hire. New York, N.Y.: AMACOM. Retrieved from http://library.gcu.edu:2048/login?url=http://search.ebscohost.com.library.gcu.edu:2048/login.aspx?direct=true&db=nlebk&AN=1919&site=eds-live&scope=site

Risavy, S. D., & Hausdorf, P. A. (2011). Personality testing in personnel selection: Adverse impact and differential hiring rates. International Journal Of Selection & Assessment, 19(1), 18-30. doi:10.1111/j.1468-2389.2011.00531.x

Arendasy, M., Sommer, M., Herle, M., Schützhofer, B., & Inwanschitz, D. (2011). Modeling effects of faking on an objective personality test. Journal Of Individual Differences, 32(4), 210-218. doi:10.1027/1614-0001/a000053

Gibson, W.M., Weiner, J.A. (2000). Practical effects of faking on job applicant attitude test scores. Retrieved from http://corporate.psionline.com/pdfs/Faking.pdf

Wooldridge, M.B., & Shapka, J. (2012). Playing with technology: Mother-toddler interaction scores lower during play with electronic toys. Journal of Applied Developmental Psychology, 33(5), 211-218. http://dx.doi.org/10.1016/j.appdev.2012.05.005

Green, James Dakota (2011). Matching organization personality perceptions and the job applicant's personality: a correlational study. PSU McNair Scholars Online Journal: Vol. 5: Iss. 1, Article 14. Retrieved from http://pdxscholar.library.pdx.edu/mcnair/vol5/iss1/14

O'Neill, T., Lee, N., Radan, J., Law, S., Lewis, R., & Carswell, J. (2013). The impact of "non-targeted traits" on personality test faking, hiring, and workplace deviance. Personality And Individual Differences, 55(2), 162-168. Retrieved from http://library.gcu.edu:2048/login?url=http://search.ebscohost.com/login.aspx?direct=true&db=edswss&AN=000319091900015&site=eds-live&scope=site

Caldwell, C., Thornton III, G. C., & Gruys, M. L. (2003). Ten classic assessment center errors: challenges to selection validity. Public Personnel Management, 32(1), 73. Retrieved from http://library.gcu.edu:2048/login?url=http://search.ebscohost.com.library.gcu.edu:2048/login.aspx?direct=true&db=bth&AN=9808263&site=eds-live&scope=site

Sutton, A., & Watson, S. (2013). Can competencies at selection predict performance and development needs?. Journal Of Management Development, 32(9), 1023-1035. doi:10.1108/JMD-02-2012-0032

Catano, V. M., Darr, W., & Campbell, C. A. (2007). Performance appraisal of behavior-based competencies: a reliable and valid procedure. Personnel Psychology, 60(1), 201-230. doi:10.1111/j.1744-6570.2007.00070.x

Hedricks, C. A., Robie, C., & Oswald, F. L. (2013). Web-based multisource reference checking: An investigation of psychometric integrity and applied benefits. International Journal Of Selection And Assessment, 21(1), 99-110. doi:10.1111/ijsa.12020

Wilson, K. Y., & Jones, R. G. (2008). Reducing job-irrelevant bias in performance appraisals: compliance and beyond. Journal Of General Management, 34(2), 57-70. Retrieved from http://library.gcu.edu:2048/login?url=http://search.ebscohost.com/login.aspx?direct=true&db=bth&AN=35882387&site=eds-live&scope=site

Stepanovich, P. L. (2013). Pernicious Performance Appraisals: A Critical Exercise. Journal Of Behavioral & Applied Management, 14(2), 107-139. Retrieved from http://library.gcu.edu:2048/login?url=http://search.ebscohost.com/login.aspx?direct=true&db=bth&AN=86206916&site=eds-live&scope=site

Huff-Eibl, R., Voyles, J. F., & Brewer, M. M. (2011). Competency-based hiring, job description, and performance goals: The value of an integrated system. Journal Of Library Administration, 51(7/8), 673-691. doi:10.1080/01930826.2011.601270

Morrow, C. C., Jarrett, M., & Rupinski, M. T. (1997). An investigation of the effect and economic utility of corporate-wide training. Personnel Psychology, 50(1), 91-119. Retrieved from http://library.gcu.edu:2048/login?url=http://search.ebscohost.com.library.gcu.edu:2048/login.aspx?direct=true&db=bth&AN=9703303255&site=ehost-live&scope=site

Siniscalco, G. R., Rahm, R. H., & Quinn, S. M. (2002). Adverse impact liability for age discrimination. Employee Relations Law Journal, 28(3), 75. Retrieved from http://library.gcu.edu:2048/login?url=http://search.ebscohost.com.library.gcu.edu:2048/login.aspx?direct=true&db=bth&AN=8855085&site=eds-live&scope=site

Mhedhbi, I. (2013). Identifying the relationship between intellectual capital and value creation of the company using structural equations analysis- the case of Tunisia. Journal Of Business Studies Quarterly, 5(2), 216-236. Retrieved from http://library.gcu.edu:2048/login?url=http://search.ebscohost.com/login.aspx?direct=true&db=bth&AN=93458517&site=eds-live&scope=site

Huffcutt, A. I., Roth, P. L., Conway, J. M., & Stone, N. J. (2001). Identification and meta-analytic assessment of psychological constructs measured in employment interviews. Journal Of Applied Psychology, 86(5), 897-913. doi:10.1037//0021-9010.86.5.897

Hogue, M., Levashina, J., & Hang, H. (2013). Will i fake it? The interplay of gender, machiavellianism, and self-monitoring on strategies for honesty in job interviews. Journal Of Business Ethics, 117(2), 399-411. doi:10.1007/s10551-012-1525-x

Stack, E. M. (2013). A new split on old age: preclusion of § 1983 claims and the adea. Fordham Law Review, 82(1), 331. Retrieved from http://library.gcu.edu:2048/login?url=http://search.ebscohost.com.library.gcu.edu:2048/login.aspx?direct=true&db=edo&AN=91690473&site=eds-live&scope=site

Winrow, B. P., & Johnson, K. (2011). Out with the old; the termination of the mixed motive case under the adea. Journal Of Legal, Ethical & Regulatory Issues, 14(1), 101-112. Retrieved from http://library.gcu.edu:2048/login?url=http://search.ebscohost.com/login.aspx?direct=true&db=bth&AN=64876656&site=eds-live&scope=site

Barrick, M. R., Dustin, S. L., Giluk, T. L., Stewart, G. L., Shaffer, J. A., & Swider, B. W. (2012). Candidate characteristics driving initial impressions during rapport building: Implications for employment interview validity. Journal Of Occupational & Organizational Psychology, 85(2), 330-352. doi:10.1111/j.2044-8325.2011.02036.x

Jansen, A., Melchers, K. G., Lievens, F., Kleinmann, M., Brändli, M., Fraefel, L., & König, C. J. (2013). Situation assessment as an ignored factor in the behavioral consistency paradigm underlying the validity of personnel selection procedures. Journal Of Applied Psychology, 98(2), 326-341. doi:10.1037/a0031257

Kleinmann, M., & Klehe, U. (2011). Selling Oneself: Construct and Criterion-Related Validity of Impression Management in Structured Interviews. Human Performance, 24(1), 29-46. doi:10.1080/08959285.2010.530634

Ajila, C. O., & Okafor, L. (2012). Employment testing and human resource management. IFE Psychologia, 20(2), 91-98. Retrieved from http://library.gcu.edu:2048/login?url=http://search.ebscohost.com.library.gcu.edu:2048/login.aspx?direct=true&db=a9h&AN=78093789&site=eds-live&scope=site

Sangmook, K. (2012). Does person-organization fit matter in the public sector? Testing the mediating effect of person-organization fit in the relationship between public service motivation and work attitudes. Public Administration Review, 72(6), 830-840. doi:10.111/j.1540-6210.2012.02572.x

Judge, T.A., Higgins, C.A., & Cable, D.M. (2000). The employment interview: A review of recent research and recommendations for future research. Human Resource Management Review, 10(4), 383-406.

Recruitment and selection policy at the ILO. (2014). Retrieved May 27, 2014, from http://www.ilostaffunion.org/new/?page_id=2635

Schmidt, F. L., Shaffer, J. A., & Oh, I. (2008). Increased accuracy for range restriction corrections: implications for the role of personality and general mental ability in job and training performance. Personnel Psychology, 61(4), 827-868. doi:10.1111/j.1744-6570.2008.00132.x

Brown, N., Pratt, Y., Woodside, L., Carraher, S. M., & Cash, R. (2009). The big five personality factors and their impact on customer services in the USA and Switzerland. Allied Academies International Conference: Proceedings Of The Academy Of Marketing Studies (AMS), 14(1), 1-5. Retrieved from http://library.gcu.edu:2048/login?url=http://search.ebscohost.c

om.library.gcu.edu:2048/login.aspx?direct=true&db=bth&AN=41529722&site=eds-live&scope=site

Lounsbury, J. W., Foster, N., Carmody, P. C., Kim, J., Gibson, L. W., & Drost, A. W. (2012). Key personality traits and career satisfaction of customer service workers. Managing Service Quality, 22(5), 517-536. doi:10.1108/09604521211281404

Kernbach, S. T., & Schutte, N. N. (2003). Emotional Intelligence of service providers as a determinant of transaction-specific customer satisfaction. Australian Journal Of Psychology, 55, 188-189. Retrieved from http://library.gcu.edu:2048/login?url=http://search.ebscohost.com.library.gcu.edu:2048/login.aspx?direct=true&db=a9h&AN=11893508&site=eds-live&scope=site

McCarthy, J. M., Van Iddekinge, C. H., Lievens, F., Kung, M., Sinar, E. F., & Campion, M. A. (2013). Do candidate reactions relate to job performance or affect criterion-related validity? A multistudy investigation of relations among reactions, selection test scores, and job performance. Journal Of Applied Psychology, 98(5), 701-719. doi:10.1037/a0034089

Magidson, J. F., Roberts, B. W., Collado-Rodriguez, A., & Lejuez, C. W. (2014). Theory-driven intervention for changing personality: Expectancy value theory, behavioral activation, and conscientiousness. Developmental Psychology, 50(5), 1442-1450. doi:10.1037/a0030583

Marcia, J. (2006). Ego identity and personality disorders. Journal Of Personality Disorders, 20(6), 577-596. Retrieved from http://library.gcu.edu:2048/login?url=http://search.ebscohost.com/login.aspx?direct=true&db=ccm&AN=2009381748&site=eds-live&scope=site

Primi, R., Ferreira-Rodrigues, C.F., & Carvalho, L. (2014). Cattell's personality factor questionnaire (cpfq): Development and preliminary study. Paidéia (Ribeirão Preto), 24(57). Retrieved from http://library.gcu.edu:2048/login?url=http://search.ebscohost.com/login.aspx?direct=true&db=edssci&AN=edssci.S0103.863X2014000100029&site=eds-live&scope=site

Ryckman, R. M. (2013). Theories of personality (10th ed.). Belmont, CA: Wadsworth.

Shaver, P. R., & Mikulincer, M. (2005). Attachment theory and research: Resurrection of the psychodynamic approach to personality. Journal Of Research In Personality, 39(1), 22-45. doi:10.1016/j.jrp.2004.09.002

Taylor, E. (1998). Jung before Freud, not Freud before Jung: the reception of Jung's work in American psychoanalytic circles between 1904 and 1909. Journal Of Analytical Psychology, 43(1), 97. Retrieved from http://library.gcu.edu:2048/login?url=http://search.ebscohost.com/login.aspx?direct=true&db=a9h&AN=3251604&site=eds-

Cam, F., Colakoglu, M., Tok, I., Tok, I., Kutlu, N., & Berdeli, A. (2010). Personality traits and DRD4, DAT1, 5-HT2A gene polymorphisms in risky and non-risky sports participation. Turkiye Klinikleri Journal Of Medical Sciences, 30(5), 1459-1464. doi:10.5336/medsci.2009-14839

Georgakopoulou, I. (2013). Psychodynamic-cognitive therapy: Working from the framework of a multimodal matrix of contributors to personality development and behavior. Journal Of Psychotherapy Integration, 23(4), 359-372. doi:10.1037/a0034361

Hocutt, M. (2013). The fruits and fallacies of Fred Skinner on freedom. Independent Review, 18(2), 263-278 Retrieved from http://library.gcu.edu:2048/login?url=http://search.ebscohost.com.library.gcu.edu:2048/login.aspx?direct=true&db=bth&AN=90025200&site=eds-live&scope=siteMagidson, J. F.,

Roberts, B. W., Collado-Rodriguez, A., & Lejuez, C. W. (2014). Theory-driven intervention for changing personality: Expectancy value theory, behavioral activation, and conscientiousness. Developmental Psychology, 50(5), 1442-1450. doi:10.1037/a0030583

Ponterotto, J. G., Ruckdeschel, D. E., Joseph, A. C., Tennenbaum, E. A., & Bruno, A. (2011). Multicultural personality dispositions and trait emotional intelligence: An exploratory study. Journal Of Social Psychology, 151(5), 556-576. doi:10.1080/00224545.2010.503718

Rennie, D. L. (2012). Occluded humanistic qualitative research: Implications for positive psychology. Humanistic Psychologist, 40(2), 166-178. doi:10.1080/08873267.2012.643692

Rich Jr., J. D. (2011). The use of pecuniary incentives for academic performance. Journal Of Applied Global Research, 4(11), 35-43. Retrieved from http://library.gcu.edu:2048/login?url=http://search.ebscohost.com/login.aspx?direct=true&db=a9h&AN=94267063&site=eds-live&scope=site

Saville, P. D., Bray, S. R., Ginis, K., Cairney, J., Marinoff-Shupe, D., & Pettit, A. (2014). Sources of self-efficacy and coach/instructor behaviors underlying relation-inferred self-efficacy (RISE) in recreational youth sport. Journal Of Sport & Exercise Psychology, 36(2), 146-156. Retrieved from http://library.gcu.edu:2048/login?url=http://search.ebscohost.com.library.gcu.edu:2048/login.aspx?direct=true&db=s3h&AN=95295174&site=eds-live&scope=site

Weiner, B. (2010). The development of an attribution-based theory of motivation: A history of ideas. Educational Psychologist, 45(1), 28-36. doi:10.1080/00461520903433596

Withers, J. (2012). The social construction of nature and Oliver Stone's natural born killers. Journal Of Popular Culture, 45(3), 649-662.

Retrieved from http://library.gcu.edu:2048/login?url=http://search.ebscohost.com.library.gcu.edu:2048/login.aspx?direct=true&db=ofs&AN=76170478&site=eds-live&scope=site

www.ingramcontent.com/pod-product-compliance
Lightning Source LLC
Chambersburg PA
CBHW062005200326
41519CB00017B/4683
9781941435083